"So many books on marriage are fog-bound in abstractions and untested theories. *Making Your Marriage Work* is a volume that real married couples can read and really benefit from. Three cheers for Christopher Reilly!"

Mitch and Kathy Finley
authors of *Christian Families in the Real World*

*"Making Your Marriage Work* makes a strong statement for viable ways to construct, inspire, and maintain healthy, ongoing marriages. Christopher Reilly brings some thirty years of experience in private counseling and psychotherapy to this practical, highly readable volume and clarifies 'what makes a good marriage.' This book is also ideal for personal reading and sharing with one's spouse, and makes an excellent gift for those contemplating marriage."

International Marriage Encounter

"Unlike the majority of marriage books with which we are blessed today, this book is not clinical and it does not stress personality-delving. It is written by a marriage counselor from a counseling, rather than a therapy, point of view: just plain old advice based on the experiences of couples who have made their marriages work....It is a very helpful, sound, usable book which every married couple would do well to read several times each year. It would also make an excellent present."

Larry Losoncy
*Marriage and Family Living*

"Reilly's self-help book is based on simple, fundamental approaches that are often overlooked in marriages, often with undesirable consequences. The author stresses the importance of good listening and communication skills, and drives home how a simple action such as laughter, or a hug or kiss, can go a long way in making life a little brighter during times of duress."

Debra A. Aleksinas
*The Litchfield County Times*

"Using a positive approach, Reilly describes attitudes and behavior that people in quality marriages demonstrate consistently. Couples from newlyweds to golden agers will enjoy the good sense and humor in this book aptly subtitled, 'Growing in Love After Falling in Love.'"

Pat Durbin
*Catholic Times*

"Reilly makes numerous suggestions in his book, suggestions about complimenting one another, laughing, erasing memories of hurts, getting down to brass tacks with each other, listening, being one-minute managers, putting your cards on the table. I'll make a suggestion, too. Get this little paperback and make it your summer project as a couple. It is down-to-earth and practical."

*Eastern Oklahoma Catholic*

"Reilly reminds his readers that 'marriages never have it made.' He emphasizes that the marital relationship is an 'ongoing proces—a growth-filled phenomenon rather than an end-event.'"

*The Catholic Transcript*

"A licensed marriage and family therapist talks about working at love, creating it anew by communicating, accommodating and understanding. Many personal stories mixed in with difficult preconceptions about marriage. Stress management. One of the better self-help books. To be used as a reference source, a 'primer' on marriage....Written with humor and a most gentle awareness of love's dangers."

*The Book Reader*

"A licensed psychotherapist, Reilly has devoted much of his practice to marriage counseling. He draws from these cases and his own marriage to illustrate many of his points in the book....The author has a very pleasant and easy-to-read style of writing and a sense of humor. In fact, he stresses the importance of humor in a marriage....Reilly also advises people not to expect to be constantly happy in their marriages. He states that unhappiness and neutral feelings are part of a relationship....He suggests that people should pursue happiness but realize that it is not something that is constant or permanent."

Peggy Weber
*Catholic Observer*

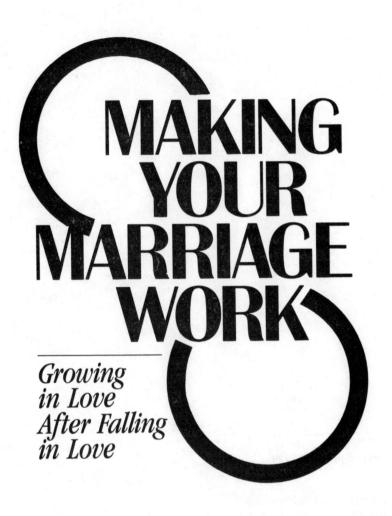

# MAKING YOUR MARRIAGE WORK

*Growing in Love After Falling in Love*

## Christopher C. Reilly

XXIII
TWENTY-THIRD PUBLICATIONS
Mystic, Connecticut

**Second printing 1990**

Twenty-Third Publications
185 Willow Street
PO Box 180
Mystic CT 06355
(203) 536-2611

ISBN: 0-89622-387-6
Library of Congress Catalog Card Number: 88-51813

# Dedication

To my wife, Kathleen,
who has taught me so much
about how to love after falling in love.

# Preface

*Making Your Marriage Work* is a "primer" on marriage that deals with the fundamental attitudes and basic behavior that couples need to practice in order to develop a quality relationship. Although it is primarily written for people contemplating marriage and those who are beginning their marital lives together, any couple seeking to enhance their conjugal relationship can profit from reading this book.

*Making Your Marriage Work* does not reveal any newly-discovered, sophisticated human relations technology, nor any scientific marriage management theories or practices, nor any state-of-the-art magic or "miracle working" that would insure a foolproof way to maintain a satisfying and lasting marriage. Nor does this book treat specific issues related to married life, e.g., finances, in-laws, sexual relations, drug and alcohol abuse, working wives, etc. There is already an abundance of these helpful books.

What this volume does reveal, however, is a simple, uncomplicated, de-mystified approach to marital success that is as "nitty-gritty" and "nuts and bolts" as you can get. It is an approach that far outweighs any specific issue in importance or value because it is the "stuff" with which any issue, regardless of its nature, is resolved. For example: If a husband and wife are ineffective in their listening skills, it really doesn't matter whether the issue to be resolved has to do with in-laws, sexual relations, etc. Their chances of successfully resolving the problem are poor to nil. (Listening effectively is one of the basic communication skills covered in this book.)

Almost thirty years of counseling married couples in trouble and an equal number of years closely associated with couples enjoying quality marriages have convinced me that we must go beyond the myth of conjugal love we hold so dearly by going back to the basics, the abc's of human love.

Couples in trouble come to counseling looking for some quick panacea that will heal their relationship. When they hear me speaking to them about how to forgive, how to accommodate, how to laugh, how to touch, etc., some find my approach too simple, too obvious, too devoid of flair and drama. One young husband, after listening to several of my suggestions, blurted out, "I'm paying you to tell me things I know already!" I quietly replied, "If you know them, what is preventing you from doing them? After all, that is why your marriage is in trouble."

Couples in trouble are neglecting the basics of healthy relating. Couples in quality marriages are attending to these basics. That, believe it or not, is the difference.

Interestingly enough, a friend who reviewed the manuscript casually commented that "if people are hung up about whether or not to divorce, they ought to read your book. Then the decision will be easy. Either they'll understand they need to go back to the basics and willingly do so, or they'll realize that if they don't want to, it's time to call it quits!" So maybe this book can also be of some service to people in such decision-making predicaments as my friend described. Of course, I would hope to see such a person opt to go back to the basics. If not, I would hope that in his or her next relationship the basics, as discussed in this book, would be more a part of his marital life.

It is amazing how a basic thing like laughing off your spouse's need to hang her freshly washed pantyhose over the shower rod can enhance the quality of your relationship!

# Acknowledgments

I thank all those married couples who have demonstrated to me over the years what quality relationships are all about.

A special debt of gratitude goes to Linda Di-Cicco, my ever-patient and enthusiastic secretary and typist, for her persevering efforts in helping to make this book a reality.

# Contents

PART TWO

BASIC BEHAVIORS

# MAKING YOUR MARRIAGE WORK
## Growing in Love After Falling in Love

# Introduction

There are two types of marriages. One is called a quality marriage, and the other is called a wounded marriage.

Wounded marital relationships can be further subdivided into mortally wounded and critically wounded. Obviously, a mortally wounded marriage is terminal and cannot be saved. A critically wounded relationship, however, can be healed and can most certainly grow into a quality conjugal union.

What makes the difference? Two factors: wanting to, and knowing what to do and how to do it. In a mortally wounded marriage, the first factor is absent. Either one or both spouses have no desire, no motivation, no commitment to work at the relationship. In essence, the marriage is dead. May it rest in peace.

In the second case, the commitment is present. It may be very strong or very weak, but there is at least the spark of motivation. The second factor, knowing how to grow a quality marriage, is absent or quite sparse at best.

Education, in the form of awareness training and behavior modification, is the recommended treatment. A wounded marriage can be healed, and a wounded marriage healed is a quality marriage. Healing a wounded marriage is actually the process of growing a quality marriage.

This book is about growing quality marriages, not ideal marriages, mind you, but quality marriages.

I could never write a book about growing ideal marriages because they really don't exist, except in the minds and hearts of our poets, songwriters, and storytellers. Writing about quality marriages, however, is another matter. They do exist and in spite of the depressing statistics related to marital and family breakdown, quality marriages are thriving in North America. They exist in abundance.

Over the past thirty years or so, I have encountered countless couples growing quality marriages, that is, mutually satisfying and lasting marriages. I have studied how they do whatever it is that enables them to enjoy satisfying and lasting relationships; others, though, suffer such grief and heartache in their struggle to find happiness.

I use the terms "growing" and "to grow" in reference to these quality marriages to reinforce two key attitudes people in these types of relationships have about marriage itself. The first is that to have a satisfying and lasting marriage requires an ongoing commitment to work together at the relationship. These husbands and wives are convinced that a conjugal relationship cannot survive, let alone bring satisfaction and stability to a couple, unless both spouses are fully aware of the need to continually attend to and nurture their union, just as a devoted horticulturist must attend to and nurture a garden.

The second key attitude that partners in quality marriages have is that growing such a relationship is never-ending. The job is never done. In this sense, they are process oriented in their outlook on marriage. They "cast very little in concrete" because they realize that the only constant in life is inconsistency, that all things change, and that movement is the basis of reality. In other words, what appears final and fixed today becomes uncertain and unstable tomorrow, in spite of all our efforts to the contrary. Today's solution may become tomorrow's problem.

These two attitudes often allow couples in quality marriages to avoid, or at least deal better with, the frustration, disillusionments, and disappointments resulting from unfulfilled expectations, broken promises, painful conflicts, and fragile solutions. These attitudes are the internal sources of the determination, cohesiveness, and mutual accommodation I have found in these quality relationships.

Surprisingly enough, many of these relationships have found their way into my counseling office (and those of my colleagues) to a point where I am convinced that 75 percent of the disturbed marriages that seek therapy are actually or potentially quality marriages looking for some help in growing their relationships, whether they are first, second, or even third marriages.

So many of these couples in trouble are horticulturists searching for more effective ways to nurture their marriages to fruition.

Whether in or out of counseling, couples growing quality marriages are not only "hearers of the word, but doers also." They act. As one couple explained, "We frequently say we love each other, and that is something we both enjoy tremendously; but we also show each other our love, and that is really where it is at."

The all too familiar, "If you love me, you will..." is often cited by authorities in the field of marriage and family therapy as a manipulative effort by one partner to persuade the other to do something he or she is hesitant or unwilling to do. A variation on this theme is: "Show me you love me by doing...."

No doubt these authorities are quite justified in their appraisal of such attempts to influence a spouse. However, there is more than a germ of truth in these quasi-demands. Love does indeed demand demonstration, not necessarily "doing what I want you to do, regardless of how you feel" approach, but most assuredly doing, acting, behaving in ways that express care, concern, respect, acceptance, understanding, pride, delight, and all the myriad feelings, sentiments, and thoughts that go into the potion we call conjugal love.

People in quality marriages are active lovers; they show their love for each other. They know that while love originates within, it must be expressed externally, or it is meaningless to the beloved.

What fascinates me, and is the subject of most of this book, is how these couples *express their love.* They would be the first to condemn the "If you love me, you will take us all to the zoo on Saturday" routine. But they would heartily agree with "If you love me, you will listen to me, you will speak honestly and congruently with me, you will problem solve with me, you will praise me and encourage me, you will forgive and honor me, you will...as I will do to you."

Each chapter of this book addresses a specific attitude or behavior that people in quality marriages demonstrate consistently. Taken all together, these chapters offer a blueprint for a mutually satisfying and lasting marriage, regardless of the context in which a conjugal relationship exists.

Perhaps that is really the secret to a quality marriage. It is not so much *what* is happening (context), as it is *how* (process) to manage the relationship. Contexts can fool us if we are not perceptive enough. In effect, no matter what is happening in a relationship, there are certain things that must be done if the marriage is to grow.

# PART ONE

# FUNDAMENTAL
# CONVICTIONS

## CHAPTER ONE

# When the Magic Is Gone

Some people fall in love; some do not. Some people fall in love more than once; some do not. Some people marry when they fall in love; some do not. Some people fall in love after they marry; some never do.

An interesting thing about falling in love is that it's effortless. It requires no output of mental or physical energy, no labor or worry whatsoever. That all comes after the fact!

Another interesting thing: Either it happens or it doesn't happen. You can't plan it. It's as simple as that!

Take my own case, for example. I met my wife Kate at a racetrack some eighteen years ago. We played the daily double together and won. It was her first trip to a track and the first time we laid eyes upon each other. She was a twenty-three-year-old elementary school teacher who, together with several other female teachers in her school, had been invited by the principal and his wife to spend an afternoon at the race track.

As a friend of the principal and also his former colleague, I was also invited to join the group in the club house. There must have been a half-dozen or so teachers present, but my attention immediately focused upon Kate. I singled her out and spent a very pleasant afternoon catering to her obvious coquettish demands.

Her charm, her wit, her attractiveness distracted me no end. By evening I knew I had fallen in love with her. I was also convinced she was at least "very fond" of me.

Falling in love with Kate was effortless. There was no deliberate, premeditated, conscious effort on my part to fall in love with her. While driving to the race track, I did not decide, "Oh, today is the day! I'm going to work at falling in love with someone at the track." Nor when I initially met Kate did I go inside myself and declare, "Yes, yes, I will now put plan A into action," alert my falling-in-love sub-systems within me, and proceed to do so. It just happened, that's all! I could only respond to the experience, after the fact, that is.

The term "to fall" aptly describes this human phenomenon, which is as consciously accidental as falling down a flight of stairs or off a horse. Ordinarily, one does not voluntarily do things like this...it just happens...like falling in love.

To fall in love, then, is not a wilful act involving a premeditated choice. It takes no energy, no effort, no work as one psychologist friend recently observed, "No blood, sweat, or tears is needed to fall in love. It is an ecstatic experience that comes on its own, needing no help from the smitten one. Cupid's arrow through the heart accurately expresses the victimlike aspect of this experience, a certain helplessness, a puzzling inability to control an inevitable surrender to the "us-ness" of the event. 'Yes, I am in love.' "

When I met Kate, I was already in the throes of trying to make a decision about my professional future. Meeting her complicated the issue quite a bit, and at the same time, moved me toward an earlier resolution of my dilemma.

Shortly after our race track encounter, I admitted to myself that I was indeed in love with Kate. I also confessed it to my psychotherapist, who was anything but impressed. I got no sympathy from him. He told me to stick to my knitting and stop complicating my already complicated situation.

I tried to take his advice. Several months passed without any attempt to contact her...months in which I painfully experienced a certain helplessness in regard to my thoughts, a puzzling inability to control my feelings, and a gradual surrender to what I really wanted with all my heart and soul. I called her, bluntly told her I was in love with her, and that I wanted to see her again. We began to see a great deal of each other from that time on. We both had fallen in love.

One can't go to school to learn how to fall in love. There are no courses treating this subject, no behavioral training or skill-building workshops available. And yet, this phenomenon is the most powerful force known to humankind. It has started wars and ended them. It is the generator of unspeakable happiness and the instigator of indescribable pain. With all our technological advances, however, we have been unable to harness the experience of falling in love! Whence originates this experience? No one actually knows; you cannot put it under a laboratory microscope and identify every piece that goes into this experience. There are some theories, of course, some more plausible than others.

In his excellent work, *The Road Less Traveled*, Dr. M. Scott Peck states that, while he does not know what this matter of falling in love is all about, he suspects that "it is a genetically determined instinctual component of mating behavior...which serves to increase the probability of sexual pairing and bonding, so as to enhance the survival of the species."[1]

Another psychoanalyst, Ignace Lepp, writing on the psychology of love, claims that it is useless to try to explain the birth of love in terms of a single driving force. "Generally," he writes, "it is a whole ensemble of causes and a set of extremely complex motivations that serve to ignite the fire of love."[2]

Perhaps the most inane question we could ever ask a person who has fallen in love is "Why?" As Dr. Lepp goes on to say, "Since unconscious motivations seem to outweigh by far the conscious motives of an individual, the subject himself is almost never in a position to tell us why he loves one particular person."[3]

I asked myself that question a thousand and one times during those months. I struggled to go on living without contact with Kate. "Why, why, why did you do such an asinine thing? Why, why, why did you let yourself fall in love?"

And the answer kept coming back to me. "I don't know why. Maybe it was this or maybe it was that, or perhaps it was this and that and probably more!"

Eric was a counseling client of mine. He *thought* he knew what kind of woman he wanted to fall in love with and marry. More than once he confided his specifications to me. She must be physically attractive, dark, petite, intelligent, ambitious, resourceful, independent, yet needful, athletically inclined, and capable of moving about comfortably within his circle of affluent friends. Above all else, she must be willing to share his values and goals. Sound somewhat macho and self-serving? Perhaps so, but at least he was honest and more in touch with his own needs than many others.

During his "bachelorhood days" he dated any number of women who more or less matched his expectations, yet none stole his heart away. Guess who he finally married? Angie, his best friend's kid sister! What was she like? Well, Angie was an attractive brunette, exceptionally intelligent, a mite taller than a classic petite usually is, and decidedly needful. She was the victim of a tragic automobile accident that left her a paraplegic. It also left her more than hesitant to mix with people socially and caused her to struggle with periodic bouts of depression.

How does one explain Eric's falling in love with Angie? His answer was certainly less than revealing. As he occasionally explained after they were married, "I don't know. It just happened that way!"

It just happened that way. In Eric's case, it was a gradual happening. He had known Angie for years. As he reports it, about a year or so prior to their marriage, he began to find himself preoccupied with thoughts of Angie. Eventually, he admitted to himself that he had fallen in love with her.

In my own case, however, it was quite sudden. I came, I saw, I fell in love with Kate! Suzanne and Jeffrey had a similar experience. They met at Jeffrey's company picnic. By the next weekend, they had fallen in love. They were married within the year.

While falling in love is effortless and requires no work or output of energy, *growing in love is work. It takes continual effort, and demands an on-going output of concentrated energy.* And this is precisely where many people get fooled! They not only fall in love, they fall for the "myth of romantic love," as Dr. Peck refers to it.[4] They convince themselves that the ecstatic experience of falling in love will last a lifetime. They believe the intensity of their love and the erotic fervor of their passion will overcome all conflict and sweep away all obstacles to their perpetual happiness. They deceive themselves into thinking that this falling-in-love kind of love will protect their relationship from the batterings of life's realities.

Many couples who are involved in wounded marriages suffer from this false conviction. They come to counseling severely disillusioned and disappointed because their experience of falling in love has gradually dissipated and left them in a painful state of confusion.

In a sense, they feel betrayed. As one young husband expressed it, "This marriage business ain't stackin' up to the way it's supposed to be!" His expectations were not being met, and he was at a loss as to what to do.

How many times in my premarital courses I have emphasized the futility and inevitable disappointment couples experience as a result of entering into marriage with these unrealistic expectations. For the most part, my well-meaning words of caution fall upon deaf ears and understandably so, for who wants to hear the "bad news" while they are so involved enjoying the "good news"? They are in love! I come over as an ogre of sorts on occasion, and I'm certain there are those in the audience who would "kill the messenger" if they dare.

This urge to kill the messenger is shared by even greater numbers in attendance when I suggest that every couple who falls in love eventually and inevitably falls out of love. We all know the hackneyed expression, "when the honeymoon is over." There is a great deal more truth than fiction in that expression. Sooner or later, the honeymoon is over, and the exciting love that merged two individuals into one begins to take second place to the business of living.

Would that it were otherwise, but no one escapes the passing nature of this experience. Why so? Again, as in the case of its coming, so with love's departure: *Who really knows?* Perhaps the best one can say is that this phenomenon of falling in love is grounded in human emotion, a more or less intense pleasurable feeling response that springs from the illusion that the lover and beloved have bridged the I-Thou gap and are truly one "in be-ing-ness."

As the illusion gradually erodes with the passage of time and life's unexpected changes, the emotion exhausts itself, leaving the lovers to face what I call the "milk pitcher syndrome" of life.

This is one of my favorite stories, probably because it's about Kate and myself approximately one year into our marriage. After all these years, it is still a painful story.

I left for work before Kate this particular day and returned to our apartment ahead of her in the late afternoon. After leisurely sorting through the mail, I wandered into our kitchen in search of something to drink and instantly spotted the milk pitcher on the counter. It was apparent Kate had forgotten to put it back in the refrigerator.

Now "Big Bird," an endearing term we sometimes used in referring to my mother, had done an excellent job in instilling in each of her three children a tiny yet powerful voice that to this day keeps repeating the axiom "waste not, want not" whenever there is the slightest danger that such might occur. Actually, that axiom makes a lot of sense if you consider the fact that we kids were born and raised during the Great Depression.

At any rate, Kate returned home a few minutes later in her usual cheery mood, only to encounter this depression baby standing in the kitchen, arms crossed, head bent in obvious disapproval, staring fixedly at the milk pitcher on the counter.

As soon as she took off her coat and walked into the kitchen, I let her have it. As best I can recall, the theme of my tirade was something to the effect that in recent months I had frequently noticed her increasing insensitivity to our financial plight, and allowing the milk to curdle and turn sour in the pitcher was proof positive that my observations were correct. What was really bugging me was that tiny yet powerful voice within me that always echoed Big Bird's drive for perfection. Kate had her back to me as I scolded her for her forgetfulness, thoughtlessness, insensitivity, etc. She slowly turned to me, tears in her eyes, her face white as a sheet, the glass of cranberry juice she had just poured shaking in her hand, and in a voice strained and barely above a whisper, spoke, "If we're going to continue to live together, you let me be myself!"

With that, she ran into the bedroom, leaving me to ponder the absurdity of my behavior the rest of the evening. It was a shattering experience for both of us. Although we had had occasional spats during our first year together, this incident marked the beginning of our falling out of love with each other. The constellation of contradictory thoughts and feelings I had that evening were mind boggling. I couldn't straighten these out into any kind of coherent logical format. Kate told me later that she was lying on the bed going through pretty much the same internal processes.

I hated myself for being so stupidly demanding, yet I was angry with her for causing me such grief. I dragged up all the garbage I had gunnysacked over the year having to do with her frequent attacks of forgetfulness. She dragged up all the garbage she had gunnysacked regarding my frequent attacks of inflexibility.

The pain, the hurt, the resentment, the disappointment, the disillusionment wouldn't subside, wouldn't go away as it had so quickly in the past after one of our spats. I began to feel a slowly growing fear, first in the pit of my stomach, then throughout my body. "Do I really love her? Did I do the right thing to marry her? What has happened to our oneness, our togetherness?"

I didn't even want to make up at that point. I had no desire as in the past to take her in my arms and tell her how much I loved her. (She felt the same way, she later told me.) She was a stranger to me that evening, and I felt so alone. The closeness was gone, and I was slipping into depression.

I didn't know what to do or which way to turn, so my unconscious took over and brought me relief. I fell asleep for an hour or so. I've been known to do that in certain stressful situations. I call it going hiding for a while. When I woke, Kate was in the kitchen preparing supper. I felt an inner calm, a peace in place of the anxiety I had experienced previously. One thought, however, kept resounding in my mind as I pulled myself up from the sofa and made my way toward the kitchen: "If we're going to make this relationship work, then we really have to begin to *work* on the relationship." It suddenly struck me, something I had read over and over a thousand times, something I had made a part of my philosophy of life, something as a marriage and family therapist I had "preached" to countless others now really made sense to me for the first time: *Marriage is a commitment to a process, an on-going process that involves a continual "working" at the relationship. It really never ends if a couple is to remain together until death!*

I began to realize in the days and weeks immediately following our shattering experience that a married relationship actually consists of three entities, two of which are already in existence, Kate and me. The third entity is brought into existence through marriage: "us-ness." Working at a marriage is doing those things that will allow you, me, and us to grow and achieve what Abraham Maslow called "self-actualization," a term he used to label the process of becoming all that one is potentially capable of becoming in this life.[5]

From this perspective, marriage is a state of existence in which two entities (man and woman) commit themselves to the lifelong process of growing a third entity, i.e., a quality relationship through which they, as individuals, and they, as a relationship, achieve their potential. And so many times it's no fun getting the three to dance together!

Fran and Al discovered this three months into their marriage. Initially, their us-ness was remarkable. Family and friends alike declared it was the closest thing to a union made in heaven they had ever witnessed. The happy couple agreed upon almost everything. Joint decision making was a snap. Each sought opportunities to sacrifice for the other. Their likes and dislikes, their needs, wants, and values were practically identical, and their goals enviably similar. They were passionately in love and inseparable. Their us-ness was never in question.

Then the "you" and "me" slowly began to assert themselves and eventually superseded the us-ness. Al wanted to move to the West Coast where his professional opportunities would be enhanced. Fran was an only child and wanted to stay in the midwest because her mother was partially incapacitated and her father was up in years.

Fran wanted to continue working as a legal secretary, while Al preferred she stop and they begin a family. He wanted to get back into league bowling, while she could not understand why he wanted to spend two nights a week at it when they could do something much more cultural and entertaining like the theater or even see a good movie together, etc. Prior to their marriage, they were aware of their value differences to some extent, but they were in love, and as Al confessed to me during our first counseling session, "Our differences didn't seem all that big."

By the time they arrived at my office, they had pretty much fallen out of love and were once again individuals, each struggling to tip the scales in their own favor. As far as Al was concerned, he was right or mostly right and Fran was wrong or mostly wrong. Fran, on the other hand, had a quite different view of matters. She was right or mostly right and he was wrong or mostly wrong!

By the time I saw them, each had collected a small cadre of well-meaning disciples who were quite liberal with their advice. Unfortunately, as in most similar situations, the advice, though helpfully intended, really did nothing more than confuse them. They were at an utter loss as to what had happened to their relationship and what could possibly be done to restore the tranquility they had so recently enjoyed.

They were stuck. What had served them well in the past, their deep and genuine feeling of us-ness, no longer was doing the job because they found it so difficult, if not impossible, to sustain that feeling. On the contrary, they were beginning to find it easier to harbor feelings of hurt and resentment, disappointment and discouragement. They had gotten to a point in the relationship where just being in neutral occasionally was a welcomed relief from the pain they were experiencing.

Fran and Al came to counseling highly motivated and at an opportune time. They dearly wanted to straighten things out. Neither one had reached the stage of apathy or indifference. Neither one had sought consolation or distraction in a third party liaison. Neither one had any inclination nor leaning toward separation or divorce.

They were ready and willing to go to work. And as the counseling progressed, they came to understand that what they had could never be restored, but what they could do would spell the difference between the success or failure of their marriage. They had fallen in love. Their individualization had taken a back seat to their us-ness for a while. Then, in the natural course of events, they had fallen out of love. The "you" and "me" (individualization) began to conflict with their us-ness, and a very painful dissonance surfaced. For Fran and Al, this happened rather early in their marriage. For Kate and myself, within a year. There is no way of determining when it will happen or how a couple will react.

Fran and Al got to work with the help of some marriage counseling. They discovered what they already knew; but until the "moment of truth," they paid mere lip service to the fact that once you fall out of love, then you are free to work at loving...*then you are free to grow a quality relationship.*

We don't like to hear this business about falling in and out of love and having to work at a relationship. We prefer to hear about and believe in romantic love, myth or no myth. We like to think that real love involves no blood, sweat, or tears. On our wedding day we gladly vow to take each other for better or for worse, for richer or poorer....At the time, these promises hold no meaning, of course. Only when we have fallen out of love, do these words come back to jolt us into reality. It is then we have to make a decision, far more serious than was the decision to marry for that matter: Do we separate, divorce, settle for a mediocre marriage, or begin to work at the relationship?

Ordinarily, we do not enter marriage with the intention of living together for a limited period of time, a year, two, or three, maybe five, at most. On the contrary, we marry with the intention of developing satisfying and lasting conjugal relationships. We seek permanence and stability in our marriage. "Till death do us part" is very much our prayerful hope, and the idea of serial monogamy is the farthest thought from our minds as we exchange our nuptial vows.

Yet our demographers predict that nationwide forty-one percent of all those people currently of marriageable age will divorce at some time in their lives. They also project that fifty percent of all first-time marriages contracted at the present time will eventually terminate in divorce. Some sociologists forecast that by 1990 there will be more remarried and single-parent homes than first-marriage nuclear families.

When we take these statistics and couple them with the fact that our national divorce rate has already accelerated three times what it was in the early 1960s, thus providing our country the dubious distinction of having the highest divorce rate in the world, the prayerful hope for a satisfying, permanent, and stable union appears to be rapidly turning into a long shot! Our divorce courts dissolve 1.2 million marriages each year. And the news takes on an even more frightening aspect when we consider that these statistics do not account for those marriages in which spouses elect to bite the bullet and remain together in mutual agony (psychological divorce).

Were these statistics also available for comparisons, we might very well conclude that growing quality marriages, i.e., mutually satisfying and lasting relationships, are in the minority in our American society.

They may be! And, if so, my fantasy is that years from now a couple who finds their first-time relationship successfully intact after thirty, forty, fifty years of marriage will be looked upon by others as belonging to *the remnant*—something that once was a given but now no longer makes sense!

There was a time when we sincerely applauded a couple on the occasion of their fiftieth wedding anniversary. We marveled at their good fortune, that the good Lord gave them health and long life together. These days, however, we seem to casually accept their blessed longevity and marvel rather at their amazing capacity to have hung in there with each other for fifty years!

So much for the not-so-good news. The good news, however, is that Fran and Al are presently enjoying a quality relationship, as Kate and myself are. And as countless other married couples are, people from every walk of life growing satisfying and lasting relationships, people we don't hear or read much about. They are the flip side of the statistical coin. I've met some (many as a matter of fact), and perhaps surprisingly so, a good many of them were by way of marriage and family counseling. They came frequently enough to enhance their relationships, not out of a deficit need to save the marriage.

While they have come from a variety of backgrounds, they have many things in common, particularly their philosophy of marriage. The conjugal relationship is of prime importance in their lives (you, me, us). They recognize and accept the fact that marriage is a never-ending process. (A couple never reaches Nirvana.) And for the process to generate a quality relationship, they are convinced a couple must continually work at the marriage.

One wife expressed her philosophy of marriage quite beautifully and so very simply at one of our conferences a short time ago. She said that she and her husband came to realize after several years together that a satisfying and lasting marriage goes beyond falling in love; once you are willing to accept this paradox, you can begin to grow in that kind of love that will bring you a quality relationship.

Perhaps if more people were of like mind and spirit, we could send our demographers and forecasters back to their drawing boards to revamp their projection downward a good bit.

An old friend of mine used to have a saying about life in general which I think can be specifically applied to the topic of marriage: "You get nothing for nothing in this life and damn little for two cents." The application is this: Quality marriages are not made in heaven. The parts may be designed there, but the relationships are manufactured, assembled, and serviced right here on earth by couples blessed with the conviction that making their relationships work means working at their relationships...continually!

Couples who are successfully growing their marriages are vitally committed to the long-term process of their relationships, to the how to of their interactions. They do not trust that their love will make all things happen magically; no more than a wise business woman trusts that her retail store will show profitability without constant management efforts on her part.

Managing a business and working at a marriage have a great deal in common. One is that they are both on-going. You never reach a point at which you can step back and say with certainty, "Well, that's it now. The business, the relationship can take care of itself from here on in." You may be able to step back and say, "Well, it's getting easier as the years go on"...maybe!

Arthur and Selma had a rude awakening forty-two years into their marriage. Just when they both felt they had it made, the proverbial roof caved in. They were embarrassed to tears when they finally came to see me at the insistence of their children. It seems that shortly after the last child left the nest, Selma began to throw herself into an ever increasing number of community and church related activities, leaving Arthur, newly retired, to pretty much fend for himself. At first he rather enjoyed the freedom to do as he pleased, to come and go as he wished. That wore off quickly, however, and he started to object to Selma's frequent absence from the home. The more he insisted upon her companionship, the more she became involved outside the home.

They were hardly speaking to each other when I initially met them. It was obvious that each felt self-righteous and at the same time guilty about their opposing points of view. Overriding everything, nevertheless, was a deeply shared disappointment that they had allowed such a situation to arise after all their years of marriage.

My immediate task was to reframe the situation in their minds and motivate them to take steps to problem solve their predicament. I suggested to them that what they were going through merely indicated to me that the relationship was alive and well, and that the you, me, and us had simply fallen out of step temporarily in the dance of life (or words to that effect). I congratulated them on the fact that their marriage was ever so real because it was obvious they were in process, and the process of growing a quality relationship is never ending.

Selma liked those thoughts instantly. Arthur was hesitant to agree at first. He was in the retirement mode. He thought that if he retired from the insurance company and all the hectic work that had involved him over the years, there should come a time when he could retire from the hectic world of raising children and learn to compromise with his spouse and sit back and enjoy the fruits of his labor.

Specifically, Arthur was talking about his dream of one day being able to travel extensively with his wife to places and sights they had denied themselves while raising their family. Selma was too busy and too satisfied with what she was doing to go any place further than their shore home. She felt a real need, almost "a calling from God" to pursue the charitable activities in which she was involved.

It took a couple of sessions to really help Arthur and Selma to let go of their disappointment at having to work through the problem at such a late date in their married lives. Once they came to terms with the fact that there is no end event in marriage, no Nirvana point at which a couple stands tall and erect upon the mountain top and proclaims, "We have it made!" they got down to work and successfully resolved the conflict.

Interestingly enough, what surfaced as the principal problem was not so much that Arthur felt isolated while Selma did her thing or even that on their own they were unable to resolve their differences, but that they had such a difference after all those years to begin with. Their mutual pride of accomplishment had been sorely wounded.

A word about the not-so-obvious. To strive for the perfect relationship in marriage is most admirable. To convince yourself that you can attain it in this life is most ludicrous. The human condition is such at this stage of human evolution that mistakes and failures are still very much a part of earthly experience.

What this means is that we can stretch the boundaries of our limitations, but we still have limitations; and one of them happens to be our penchant for inconsistency, especially in our relationships. In effect, I have yet to meet a couple who have been consistently compatible in their conjugal relationship. And no matter how long a time a couple spends together, their work is cut out for them. They will have to continually strive to maintain the balance between the you, me, and us.

Whether you are married forty-one hours or forty-one years, the process of marriage goes on. People growing quality relationships never really stop working at them. They realize that you never have it made in marriage. This position is not always obvious to some people who think that after x number of years they should be able to sit back, enjoy the ride, and put their interaction on cruise control. How taken back they are, as in the case of Arthur and Selma, when they run into traffic down the road and have to take over once again. Too often they are out of practice, so in the prime of their lives they opt to divorce, not because their problems are insurmountable, but because they forgot how to work at their marriage. They took it for granted! If you think this an exaggeration, note that in the last fifteen years the rate of divorce for people forty to sixty-five years of age has risen fifty percent.

Lest you get the impression that working at your marriage means only remedial efforts, let me correct that by telling you about Jonas and Ann, a couple in their mid-eighties. They were deeply religious individuals and daily church-goers. Each morning, weather permitting, they could be seen walking hand in hand down the street toward St. Vincent Church. After the services they would return to their home in the same manner.

Jonas and Ann were forever doing things for each other, creating delightful little surprises for each other. They had several grown children and many grandchildren, even a couple of great-grandchildren, all of whom loved them dearly. Yet it was obvious who came first in the eyes of each. I was told they had always been that way, and when I once complimented them on the extraordinary care and concern they showed for each other, Jonas simply reminded me that that was what marriage was all about, as far as he was concerned.

They were truly committed to enhancing their relationship as long as God gave them breath to do so. In myriad ways over sixty years together they had demonstrated their commitment to each other. They were indeed a couple who worked at growing a quality relationship. They died about seven months apart several years ago. Ann passed away first, then Jonas. I was privileged to be with him at his last moments. He was more than ready to go; he was so anxious to be reunited with his beloved Ann. He, for one, was convinced marriage was not until "death do us part," but rather for eternity. Just before he went into a coma and shortly thereafter passed away, he smiled up at those hovering around his bedside and weakly remarked he was certain Ann was waiting with a hundred and one chores for him to do! Who is to say that was not so?

## CHAPTER TWO

# Happiness Is a Spin-Off

It happens frequently at cocktail parties, along about the second drink and the third tray of cheese dip and unsalted crackers. I see her coming out of the corner of my eye. She approaches quietly from across the room, politely introduces herself, and quickly explains she has just discovered, by way of a mutual friend, that I am a marriage and family therapist. The inevitable question follows: "What do you think is the reason why so many people are getting divorced these days?"

When I was younger, green, more patient, and drank more, I would take to my podium and answer the question with a rather lengthy laundry list of the whys and wherefores. My list included, but was not restricted to, such sociological and cultural issues as:[1]

- modern day woman's struggle for equality
- the gradual acceptance of serial monogamy
- the painfully slow yet real transition from traditional marriage to companionship marriage

- the confusing emergence of alternative lifestyles
- the rapidly growing phenomenon of the two-career couple
- changing attitudes toward parenthood
- traditional male and female modifications.

Just to be sure I was covering all the bases, I'd usually throw in a few of the old stand-bys that have always played havoc with conjugal love and family love: alcoholism, drug abuse, infidelity, sexual incompatibility, financial stress, work stress, extended family problems, etc.

As time went by and the cocktail parties multiplied, I learned to curb my enthusiasm and shorten my response. This for several reasons. For one thing, my drink turned to water, my pipe kept going out, and my questioner always finished the cheese dip and crackers while I was immersed in my monologue.

A second reason had to do with my growing awareness that no one really wants a crash course in "Modern-Day Divorce: A Thousand and One Reasons Why" in the midst of a cocktail party. I began to notice the stifled yawns and shifting eyes.

The third reason I drastically shortened my laundry-list approach was the fact that thousands of hours devoted to the practice of marriage-couple therapy led to the obvious conclusion that regardless of the specific circumstances or particular situations of each couple, all had at least one thing in common: *They were unhappy in their marriages!* And those who chose to end their relationship did so because they saw divorce as a viable alternative to a lifetime of unhappiness.

So why bother to elaborate on the rapidly growing phenomenon of the two-career couple and its decided impact on marriage and family life, or the gradual acceptance by our society of serial monogamy and its impact on marriage and family life, or any and all the other social and cultural variables on my list, when the bottom line is that marriages break up because people reach a point on their unhappiness scale that signals the end. *Have you ever met a couple who divorced because they were happily married?*

So, in recent years, I've found myself responding to my cocktail inquisitors with the rather succinct and somewhat factitious observation: "Well, Ms. Honeywell, I have yet to meet a couple who split because they were enjoying a satisfying relationship. People divorce because they are unhappy. It seems, then, if our demographers are correct, that more and more people are unhappily married....Do you not agree?"

I admit that this response is factitious, but it is the truth! Men and women happily married do not divorce. Unhappy people do. And of course, the more unhappily married folks there are, the more divorces occur. If the available statistical data predict that fifty percent of all first-time newlyweds will eventually divorce, then what these data are really telling us is that half the current population of newlyweds will become so unhappy with their marital status they will seek relief in divorce.

We can talk all we want about those sociological and cultural issues I cited above. We can philosophize about them *ad nauseam*, identifying each of them or any combination of them as contributing to the accelerated divorce rate and the present instability of marriage. But when all is said and done, the simple, plain old, unsophisticated, and obvious fact remains: Divorce is a choice made by people who are unhappy in their marriages. And the accelerated divorce rate in our country in recent years basically says one thing. More and more unhappy people are opting for divorce!

Now, of course, the converse is just as true. People growing satisfying and lasting marriages are happy together. So what actually makes the difference? The difference has to do with any number of variables, but the variable that really makes the difference has to do with a couple's "happiness frame of reference" in relation to their marriage.

Not long ago, I sat with a young couple in a counseling session and listened while they expressed such unrealistic expectations and attitudes regarding marital happiness that I secretly marveled at the fact they had somehow managed to live together for the three years they did. The demands they were placing upon their relationship and each other in terms of providing some kind of idyllic happiness was unbelievable. No marriage, however healthy, can provide the kind and amount of happiness this couple was looking for.

I'd be the first to tag their youthfulness as the culprit except for the fact that I'm familiar with many more couples who are not so youthful, yet harbor like illusions. One woman I know is ending her marriage in the pursuit of happiness. According to her, she just hasn't found the right man yet. Evidently, Mr. Right is supposed to come along with a bag full of miraculous powers and skills that will protect her forever from such earthly demons as disappointment, frustration, boredom, anxiety, stress, depression, poor self-esteem, financial cares, and so on.

It is not difficult to understand why people have such grandiose expectations about the happiness their marriage should give them. In our North American society, at least, the name of the game is happiness. Everything we do is supposed to bring us happiness. We're constantly being bombarded with happiness propaganda. This suit will make you feel good about yourself. That house will fulfill all your dreams. This job will bring you the sense of achievement you desire. This vacation spot, that motion picture, this stage show, that book, this widget, that what-have-you will delight you no end.

It seems like everything we do is weighed on a happiness scale. I must buy my children tons of Christmas gifts so they will be happy. I must try to keep my parents happy, my husband happy, my wife happy, my in-laws happy, my friends and neighbors happy...and, of course, myself happy. Or else!

I don't know of any other nation that spends more time, money, and effort than we do planning, organizing, directing, and controlling happiness in our lives. We can't get enough of it. We are satiated with it. We are a nation of "happyholics," a society addicted to the pursuit of happiness. No wonder we enter marriage with a happiness frame of reference that, all too frequently, holds little toleration for the unhappy and even neutral aspects of everyday living.

Someone once said that if you go far enough north, you start going south, and when you go far enough south, you start going north again. I like that concept. It can be applied quite nicely to the human condition we call happiness. It comes and it goes, and it returns only to leave again and....Our apostles of happiness would have us believe that there is a constant state of happiness attainable in this life. And they have so many ways of convincing us.

That is why our streets are crowded with people walking about in various stages of depression. Depression is their grieving reaction to their inability to attain and retain the happiness level they were sold on. They were sold a sorry myth—making happiness a goal guarantees you'll achieve it—as though happiness were some object outside of oneself that one latches on to. They were promised an impossible dream: Working hard at happiness means you'll always be content. They bought a pie-in-the-sky approach to life: If you tell yourself to be happy, even taking the garbage out on a freezing January morning can be fulfilling!

Naturally, they're depressed. I'd be, too, were I to spend the time and energy they do chasing rainbows, only to find more rain. What we need is a much more balanced and realistic happiness frame of reference, especially when it comes to marriage. I am convinced, for example, that fewer people would seek divorce were they better able to tolerate those unhappy or neutral instances, situations, circumstances, etc., that arise in any normal relationship.

I noted earlier in this chapter that people dissolve their relationships because they are unhappy. I suspect that seemed a simplistic statement to many readers. At face value, it probably is, but within it is the essence of the matter regarding our accelerating divorce rate. *People can no longer tolerate unhappiness or even an emotional state of neutrality in marriage very long before questioning the very structure of their conjugal relationship.*

They come to blame their unhappiness, or better still, their lack of happiness on the relationship. What's wrong with that? Well, for one thing, they fail to consider the possibility that their happiness frame of reference is unrealistic to begin with, and what they are expecting from marriage is more than this human institution is capable of giving at this period of humankind's evolution. And for another thing, they find it difficult to understand and accept the nature of happiness itself. For example, happiness is filled with paradox. To enjoy it, we must stop trying to *secure* it as though it were some object or product to be gained.

Happiness, in or out of marriage for that matter, is a spin-off of purposeful action.[2] Blessed is the person who is a goal setter. He is very much involved with life. He is a "doer," busy about his responsibilities, duties, interests. He desires it, but is willing to let the happiness chips fall where they may. He knows happiness basically comes from a life of service, dedication, and devotion.

He also knows not to confuse it with immediate pleasure, the instant gratification syndrome affecting so many these days. He is able to postpone his need for happiness in favor of accomplishing what may often involve prolonged, and at times, painful effort on his part. The light at the end of the tunnel may be dim at times, but he perseveres because he knows his pursuit of happiness depends on his pursuit of a life that finds meaning in giving and receiving, in sacrifice and discipline, in waiting and pleasure, in restriction and freedom.

Yesterday I was relatively content and satisfied. Today I am not. I feel restless and edgy. I am experiencing another paradox of happiness: It comes and it goes. I cannot, at least in this life, hold on to it forever, as much as I want to. But I know it will return if I do not try to force it.

My task is to continue to do what I am doing and resist the temptation to "mind dwell" on the whys and wherefores of my discontent. That strategy will only anchor my discontent. Peace, calm, perhaps even the restoration of happiness, will come through my attention to the present, the here and now of the task I am now doing. Personal growth through enhanced insight and expanding awareness of one's mental and emotional processes is a commendable endeavor. Too much mind-dwelling, however, is absurd!

I know a gentleman who is slowly analyzing himself right out of his marriage. He is constantly exploring, examining, and questioning his thoughts and feelings regarding just about everything in his life, but particularly his marriage. He is a happyholic, and he is miserable. He has reached a point—no exaggeration—where he barely does anything unless he first applies his happiness criteria! "I am not happy at work so maybe I should look for another job. I'd like to go back to college, but maybe it's not worth it and I'll be sorry. I wonder if I ought to move the family into another area, but if I do, will I (they) be satisfied?"

In the meantime, he is driving his wife and children up the wall. Every suggestion she makes in his behalf is rejected, and he is seriously beginning to doubt his love for her because he doesn't find much in her to be "turned on" about. He struggles to find something in his life that will bring him happiness. The last time I heard about him, he had jumped on the merry-go-round and joined up with some other happyholics. Together, they seek out, try on, and eventually discard every opportunity for happiness. Nothing satisfies them.

His therapist sees him as a free soul, an exciting and adventurous risk taker, always anxious to experiment with life and drink the cup of fulfillment to the dregs. His wife and children think otherwise. So do I. I think he is in for big trouble if he doesn't jump off that merry-go-round. He might just keep going round and round! If you think this is an exceptional case, look again.

Ralph Waldo Emerson said that a person knows she has grown when she recognizes that the place where she has arrived is the place she started from. This is something to consider when we are tempted to pack our bags and head down the yellow brick road. The happiness we seek might very well be exactly where we are. And if we are willing to resist groping for it, and attend to what we are about, it may very well spin off right into our laps!

Genuine happiness is spontaneous, like falling in love. You can't plan it, organize it, direct it, or demand it. You can only create and manage the movement that may or may not bring it.

The quality marriages I've observed, including my own, are being grown by couples who never promised each other a rose garden, but did promise to live together in the good times and the not so good times, and let the happiness chips fall where they may.

The satisfying and lasting relationships I've observed, including my own, are also grown by couples who can live in *neutral* and be comfortable doing it, when neutral is the order of the day.

What, for heaven's sake, is living in neutral? It's what we do ninety-five percent of our day, day in and day out, and usually we don't even advert to this common emotional state. Some people translate it as unhappiness. These are the individuals who polarize their happiness spectrum, so to speak. At one end of the spectrum is happiness. At the opposite end is unhappiness! They don't see any continuum aspect to their spectrum of happiness. They see no middle ground, no neutral state wherein one is neither happy—aware of a sensation of fulfillment at the moment, nor unhappy—aware of a sensation of unfulfillment at the moment. In a neutral feeling state, one is simply not attending to any positive or negative emotions at the moment; one's psychic energies are directed elsewhere.

Some married people also confuse this neutral emotional state with apathy, or indifference. While Webster's dictionary would lead you to think they are the same, such is really not the case. As I am writing, I have no conscious sensation of happiness or unhappiness or any other feeling. I would not say, however, because I lack feeling or emotion (Webster's first definition of apathy) for what I am doing that I am therefore unconcerned (Webster's second definition of apathy) about my writing! On the contrary, I am very much interested and concerned about this chapter as I write; however, I am in a present neutral emotional state.

Ali confused this matter in her own mind some time ago. She thought because she felt little or nothing for Dan, one way or another, she was becoming apathetic and indifferent toward him. They had been married about eight years at the time I met them and had two preschool youngsters, the younger one having a congenital hip dislocation that required a good bit of Ali's attention and energies.

Dan also worked long and hard hours in his own construction business, which left very little time for him and Ali to share much needed intimate and exclusive togetherness. Get the picture? There is Dan attending to his newly created business and achieving chunks of self-achievement in the process. Ali, on the other hand, is at home attending to the household chores, as well as two extremely dependent offspring and achieving chunks of discouragement and disillusionment in the process, and feeling guilty about it on top of it all!

Ali acknowledged that Dan was a very caring and loving husband and father and helped out all he could whenever he was around. She was certain the problem was hers; she just had no feeling for him. She knew she cared about him, was concerned about his business, did for him however she could, but found it next to impossible to generate those feelings she used to have up until recently. She could not understand what she called her apathy toward him. Why, she repeatedly asked herself, did she seem indifferent to him? At least if she felt some anger or hurt or disgust, or something like that, she would say to herself, then there would be some feeling, some life in her interactions with him. But there seemed to be no feeling one way or the other!

Ali wasn't apathetic toward Dan. She wasn't in a state of disinterest or unconcern. She was in neutral at the time. Her energies were necessarily directed elsewhere for the most part, leaving her little or no surplus to direct toward Dan.

Another way to describe the situation is to use a comparison. Suppose you are comfortably seated in your family room watching an engrossing movie on TV. You are very much emotionally involved in the sequence of events and then the phone rings, and it is your mother letting you know how upset, disappointed, and hurt she was because you left her Mother's Day dinner so early. Suddenly your emotional involvement shifts to the telephone conversation, even though you are still watching the movie. You become emotionally associated with your mother's voice, and although aware of the movements and sounds of the thriller, you are emotionally separated from it. You are no longer in the picture, but a spectator as you get into the conversation with your distraught mother. Your energies are mustered to take on Mom rather than the movie villain.

In a similar fashion, yet over a much longer period of time, that is what happened to Ali. While she continued to relate to Dan, she gradually did so in a dissociated manner—neutral emotional state—because she gradually became very associated with her own predicament.

Being neutral in marriage is neither good news nor bad news in itself. Many times in the course of marital or couple therapy, I strive to move the couple from a position of unhappiness (anger, resentment, hurt, bitterness, etc.) with each other to the position of neutral before attempting to move on toward the happiness pole of the spectrum. To jump from the extreme negative pole to the extreme positive pole is too much to ask, more often than not!

It's amazing, however, how many couples begin to take charge of their own therapy when they reach that neutral state. Remember, although there may not be the emotional, satisfying sensations that accompany the happiness state at this point, neither are there the emotional, unsatisfying ones that we call unhappiness. People at this point are ready to get to work on the relationship, for they've laid aside their heavy gunnysacks filled with their garbage of the past.

As I mentioned previously, most of our daily living is done in neutral, and those people growing quality relationships know this all too well, and live with this fact quite realistically. When the happiness state dims or disappears, they don't panic and run for help. They know there is a time and place for everything. They also know that those philosophers of life who limited their views of the human condition to such bi-polar descriptions as "highs and lows," "peaks and valleys," "ups and downs," "good times and bad times," etc., failed to include in their descriptions the place where we actually spend most of our time in this life, *in neutral!*

Does all I have said mean that I am advocating we give up the quest for happiness and the eventual obliteration of all unhappiness in marriage? Not on your life! What I am advocating is that while we pursue happiness in marriage and strive to obliterate unhappiness as much as possible, we recognize and accept that happiness cannot be pursued, captured, and mounted as though it were some fair game destined to become a fixed prize in one's study; rather, we admit that happiness is a spin-off from purposeful activity within marriage, and the real pursuit lies in the efforts we expend on behalf of the conjugal relationship.

## CHAPTER THREE

# The Yin and Yang of It

Growing a quality marriage requires discipline, a certain "self-possession" that enables an individual to control his or her emotions and actions. A disciplined person does not repress emotions nor deny them, but exercises appropriate direction over them.

To some, this last statement may seem rather cold, mechanical, and computerlike. However, the truth of the matter is that an individual who controls his or her emotions is no less a feeling person than one who lives by the dictates of his or her emotions. As M. Scott Peck says:

> The fact that a feeling is uncontrolled is no indication whatsoever that it is any deeper than a feeling that is disciplined. We must not assume that someone whose feelings are modulated and controlled is not a passionate person.[1]

Passion is feeling in depth. I have a client whose wife complains that he is insensitive and unfeeling, and acts more like an automaton than a warm-blooded human being. I know this young man, clinically and personally; I know his wife's evaluation is sadly exaggerated, and I can understand why. She wants him to be more like herself. She wears her emotions on her sleeve. She evidently keeps very little to herself, expressing her innermost thoughts and feelings to friends and family alike. As far as she is concerned, she is open and honest with everyone...even when it hurts herself or others.

This woman is very attractive and has an outgoing personality. She speaks rapidly and loudly, apparently has scads of friends and is somewhat of a Perl Mesta in her community. She has also been known to have become entangled in several hot neighborhood squabbles over the years, one of which actually led to a lawsuit eventually settled out of court!

Her husband is laid back, quiet, reserved, with a splendid and insightful sense of humor. He generally speaks softly and sparsely, and is well liked by the few who take the time to get to know him. I view him as a warm-hearted man who is in control of his emotions and actions. He most decidedly does have feelings and can be quite passionate when so inclined. He is a man in possession of himself, the owner of his feelings. In my estimation, he is a self-disciplined individual, but not an automaton by any means.

Self-discipline, self-possession, emotional control, self-directed behavior are all terms that connote healthy maturity. They are also terms that have been grossly neglected and frightfully overlooked in our lexicon of daily living.

Not too long ago a good many self-dubbed social scientists were writing and speaking on the subject of open marriage. With varying degrees of seriousness, these people advocated that married couples generate "growth-filled" extramarital liaisons while remaining coupled. These intimate affairs were to be above board, known and accepted by the other spouse, hence, the open marriage concept.

Whether overt or covert, many married people, taking the

idea of having extramarital affairs to heart, as if some social license had been granted them by these dubious authorities, indulged themselves and sought out these "growth-filled" relationships, only to soon find their marriages on the rocks. It was about that time also that we began to witness a rapid acceleration in our nation's divorce statistics, a phenomenon that is still going on.

Quality marriages are not open marriages by any stretch of the imagination, nor do they tolerate any covert type of sexual intimacy with a third party. As old-fashioned and stereotyped as it may sound, growing a quality relationship leaves room only for two. That is simply the yin and yang of it. If you wish to grow such a marital union, then don't muddy the waters with overt or covert extramarital liasons.

Now that seems obvious, doesn't it? To even say it is somewhat of an insult to one's intelligence. If so, then why are a good many of the troubled couples I work with in counseling involved with third-party intimacies? And I don't mean the all too common one-night stand either. I mean the prolonged and persistent psychological, emotional, sexual, and in many cases, financial interpersonal relationship that is in actuality a quasi-marriage of its own!

How come? Because for whatever reasons, the spouse in question failed to exercise the self-discipline, the self-possession, the emotional control, the directed behavior required to avoid such an involvement.

Well, which comes first, or what prompts what? The third-party involvement causes the trouble in the marriage or trouble in the marriage precedes the involvement? I've never taken an actual head count, but I know it is realistic to say that in ninety-five percent of the cases, trouble in the marriage precedes the third-party involvement. In the other five percent, it usually is the opposite: The extramarital affair causes trouble in what, up till then, was a reasonably healthy marital relationship.

In either case, the spouse in question failed to take leadership over his or her rational emotive processes, i.e., failed to exercise self-discipline and self-possession. And that is the yin and yang of it! Regardless of the circumstances, we can control our internal processes: the way we think, feel, and act. We only become victims of our internal processes if we allow it; that is the opposite of self-discipline.

In Chapter One, I discussed the phenomenon of falling in love. I said it was involuntary and effortless. It is. That is why married people can become strongly attracted to individuals other than their spouses, whether their own marriage is intact or not. The tendency to do so, however, apparently lies with the husband or wife who has a troubled marriage. This is understandable. People in trouble reach out for understanding, consolation, and acceptance. You don't have to go far to find another person who can and will meet those needs.

Falling in love with or being strongly attracted to a person other than one's spouse is one thing. Allowing oneself to pursue such a relationship is quite another. This is an instance where self-discipline is the alternative to an extramarital affair. Ask Tony.

Tony fell in love with Roxanna. Tony was married with three children, had a handsome income as a high tech consultant, a lovely home in an affluent community, and a wife who truly enjoyed her role as a homemaker. She was perfectly comfortable leaving the bread-winning up to her husband, who totally agreed with her. They had a quality marriage and a healthy family life.

Nine years into their marriage Tony got an extremely lucrative consulting contract with a company whose home base was on the West Coast. That meant he had to spend a great deal of time away from his wife and children during the first six months of the project. Initially he commuted every other weekend from one side of the country to the other. The commuting eventually got to him, and he began to lessen his weekend trips back to the East Coast.

Just about that time, the company hired a new project manager, Roxanna; and the liaison began soon after. It only took a few project meetings between Roxanna and Tony before Tony was "blown out," as he described it. Tony fell in love with her! And Roxanna, from Tony's report, fell in love with him!

What transpired is what movies are often made of: the love, guilt, justification triangle. Tony and Roxanna were in love. The ecstasy of new and exciting intimacy flooded their beings, followed shortly by searing guilt and sporadic depression. (Both were happily married up till then to people who loved and trusted them.) They decided it was best to call it quits. Tony would keep his distance; Roxanna would do likewise.

That arrangement lasted about three days before thrice-a-day phone calls pushed them back into each other's arms. And as they sank deeper and deeper into the quagmire of their illicit love affair, they began to justify their position on two counts. They rationalized that because their feelings for each other were much stronger and more real to them than either felt for their own spouses, it was meant to be, i.e., it was their destiny, their fate to meet and fall in love. They also began to rationalize their relationship by gradually discovering through their marathon talk sessions that they really had not been all that contented and happy with their own marriages, so better to end them than go on living a lie!

Eventually, the inevitable happened and they rode off into the sunset together, leaving a trail of broken hearts and bewildered minds behind.

Adrian's story is rather similar to Tony's. Where it differs is the fact that her six years of marriage to Marty had been a living hell for both of them long before she fell in love with Irv.

Her troubled marriage set the stage, to some extent, for the role of mistress she assumed shortly after meeting Irv. She played this role for four years before they both divorced their respective spouses and took up open cohabitation. Looking back on the matter, Adrian concluded that at the time she met Irv she was terribly vulnerable to a sensitive and caring man like Irv, who instantly made her feel the self-respect and self-confidence she thought she had lost forever.

Janette's circumstances were similar to Tony's. The ending, however, was different. After two years of clandestine romancing with her amour, she gave him up and devoted all her energies to enhancing her own relationship with her husband. Unfortunately, as happens in many similar situations, they were never quite able to restore the intimacy they had previously experienced, nor realize the potential for mutual growth they once knew. They have settled for less.

We can sympathize with all those people I've mentioned and with all those good men and women who have lived similar experiences. Yet the fact remains there was an alternative each could have reached for: the choice of self-discipline and self-possession. Not an easy choice by any means, but the right choice, and really the only choice when one is committed to growing a quality marriage.

I am familiar with men and women in quality relationships who have fallen in love or have been strongly attracted to individuals other than their spouses. After all, there is no basis of truth whatsoever in the idea that the foundation of a quality relationship is grounded in psychological and sexual exclusivity, i.e., that the spouses were somehow predestined for each other and for no one else in this world! It is possible, then, to have a quality marriage and to love outside the marital relationship. Ask Marsha.

Marsha loves her husband dearly and he her, and they do have a mutually satisfying relationship, one I'm certain that will be lasting. Several years ago Marsha fell deeply in love with her graduate school mentor, a university professor twenty years her senior. At first she was beside herself with guilt and remorse, totally confused about her feelings and what she wanted to do. She was referred to me for counseling by a close friend in whom she confided her painful dilemma.

Marsha and I worked together weekly for several months to help her straighten her life out. She had so much going for her, not the least of which was her background. She was raised by a mother and father who were loving and caring parents, yet firm disciplinarians. They taught their children how to recognize and accept personal responsibility and instilled in them an intelligent and realistic self-discipline delicately balanced with a keen sense of humor and the capacity to flex when necessary.

The first thing we worked on was the matter of her guilt, self-blame, shame, and remorse. Through some insightful discussions between us and a bit of cognitive counseling, she gradually accepted the idea that her falling in love was involuntary, and though some guilt was a normal consequence, punishing herself with obsessive blame, shame, and remorse was completely uncalled for and certainly unproductive.

In conjunction with this approach, we likewise took up the problem of what to do about it. Here is where her self-discipline training came greatly to her aid. Chunk by chunk, we examined the various steps she might take to avoid what might otherwise become a dreadful tragedy for many people. It was evident that the professor in question, who was also married yet felt the same toward her, was openly pressuring her to pursue the relationship.

As difficult as it was, Marsha insisted he cooperate with her efforts to confine the relationship to those interactions related to her thesis preparation. After several half-hearted attempts to do so, they both realized this strategy would not work. Much against his will and equally distasteful to her, she dissociated herself from him by taking a sabbatical from her dissertation work under the pretense she was burned out and needed some "R and R." Actually there was very little, if any, pretense involved. She was a stress-filled young woman at the time, and this strategy was more than justified.

What to do about the phone calls and frequent correspondence? For a while she accepted the idea of a twice weekly phone call (she called him at his office) and occasional short letters or notes between them, what we might call gradual withdrawal. Then she got up enough courage to cut the phone calls to once every couple of weeks and steadfastly refused to be persuaded otherwise, not without great pain at times. She also responded to his increased and lengthy letter writing with less frequent correspondence, and shorter and less personal content, again not without great distress. After all, she did love the man! As her therapist, I made suggestions, but she was the one who had to bite the bullet and carry them through! And she did.

Perhaps the most difficult of all tasks was the internal work we had to do, controlling her thoughts and feelings about her professor, as well as her thoughts and feelings about her husband and young child. In this matter, the name of the game was self-possession, the ability and capacity to manage her internal processes.

She had to mentally and emotionally disassociate herself from her professor and intensify her mental and emotional association with her husband and child. We accomplished this to an acceptable extent only after much pain and practice on her part. She had to learn how to change those images in her mind and those things she said to herself that generated the love feelings she had for the professor. She had to replace those internal images and dialogues with images and dialogues dealing with her husband and child. She had to learn how to interrupt her own thinking, in other words, and change it in favor of her marriage and family.

The bulk of our time together was actually spent on teaching her how to do this. She stayed with it, and gradually she came to control her feelings toward the professor and her husband with more ease and surety. To this day, she still has a deep love for the professor, but it is one she no longer fears because she is in the driver's seat and is able to possess herself, which is the real meaning of self-discipline.

In telling Marsha's story, I am sometimes asked if they had had sexual relations before they broke up. The answer is no. And perhaps that fact has a lot to do with Marsha's eventual and successful dissociation from him and her continued commitment to a quality marriage. She did not allow their relationship to include sexual activity, as much as she desired it. She knew in her heart that if she made love with him the whole situation would be horribly complicated. In this instance, Marsha owned her feelings. She did not allow her emotions to drive her to the point of adultery and, quite possibly, the beginning of the end of her marriage.

Marsha's story happened several years ago. To this day, she maintains a genuine love for her professor friend. She reports they have had no contact whatsoever since he took himself and his family to another part of the country and another university. And she has gone on to successfully complete her doctoral program while enhancing her relationship with her husband and family.

Another question I am occasionally asked is: Did her husband know or even suspect Marsha was in love with another man? The answer: Yes, but not at first. In the course of our counseling, however, she decided to reveal the entire situation to him. Needless to say, he initially went into a state of semi-shock, followed by frequent fits of anger and periods of depression. Gradually he filtered out these destructive and unproductive emotions and supported her in every way possible as she worked through her ordeal. An exceptional couple? Perhaps, but without a doubt they were a couple committed to growing a quality marriage!

Is it not possible for a married man or woman to develop genuinely loving relationships outside the marriage without endangering the marriage? Evidently, there are those who can do it, but it does require a capacity for self-discipline and self-possession that most people do not possess. And that is the yin and yang of it!

It is no easy task to grow a quality marriage these days. More and more, men and women are being thrown together in the world of business and industry and required to work long hours together, endure and share stressful situations together, travel extensively together, and speak a common technical language that is usually foreign to their respective spouses. In effect, it takes a person with great self-discipline to maintain constructive relationships outside the home without jeopardizing the marriage. Ask Harry.

Harry is a junior executive with a large manufacturing organization. He and his wife Ida have been growing a quality relationship for twenty-two years. In our monthly couples' discussion group he is often the first to speak up about the need for self-discipline and, as he likes to call it, continual vigilance in the work-a-day world.

Harry is a personable, fun-loving individual who enjoys a good time. He is also an intelligent and mature husband, father, and professional who has good insight into human nature, including his own, and is quite cognizant of his strengths and weaknesses. He started in the factory, went to college at night, gradually worked his way into the management position he now has.

Harry knows what the world of business and industry is like. He knows what it can do to a marriage if a person allows himself or herself to become a victim to the pressures, illicit pleasures, and temptations that are very much a part of this world. He has time and again watched helplessly one co-worker after another destroy his or her marriage and family life through infidelity and other indiscretions.

He saw a great amount of this kind of irresponsibility during the 1970s, a decade Thomas Wolfe refers to as the Me Decade. It was a time when most people seemed to abandon loyalty, fidelity, self-sacrifice, patience, prudence, perseverance, acceptance, charity, commitment in the name of self-love and the search for one's "real identity." It was a time when great numbers of marriages disintegrated because spouses were too busy trying to "find themselves" to pay much attention to their partners, or children for that matter.

Harry is the first to admit he had his moments, too, during that period when he was sorely tempted to buy into the "I gotta be me" routine, throw caution to the wind, and join the ever-increasing number of bohemian risk-takers at work who were bouncing from one relationship to another, searching for life's true meaning and who they really were!

What prevented him from succumbing to this charade? Pretty much the same things that Marsha relied on to help her weather the storm of passion and love: discipline, self-possession, emotional control, directed behavior, and of course, a set of values that included the commitment to grow a quality marriage, regardless of the sacrifices entailed.

Does all that I have been saying imply that married people who are growing quality marriages cannot, under any circumstances, enjoy the friendship of members of the opposite sex? By no means! What I am stating unequivocally, however, is that men and women who enjoy mutually satisfying and lasting relationships have their priorities in tow and behave accordingly. They are the masters of their feelings, the managers of their emotions, the generators of their thoughts, rather than the passive recipients. They are in control of their friendships.

## Chapter Four

# It Feels Good to Laugh

*"You're only here for a short while, so have a few laughs and don't take things so seriously—especially yourself."*

**Mark Twain**

Some time ago, a new client managed to go through a full box of tissues while tearfully relating the painful story of her marriage breakup. As she struggled to find the right words to describe what happened, I quietly placed a wastepaper basket alongside her and quietly moved the tissue box on the coffee table closer to her reach. She was oblivious to what I had done, so engrossed was she in her monologue. Only when she reached for another tissue and found the box empty and instinctively looked down at the basket filled with rolled up tissue, did she suddenly stop speaking. Her eyes widened for a moment as she looked at me; then she smiled and began to laugh softly. I joined her in her laughter and we enjoyed the moment. She paused, and then said, "You know, it feels good to laugh for a change, and I'm laughing at myself! I owe you a box of tissues." I replied, "Hey, be my guest. There is no additional charge for tissue."

It always feels good to laugh. That is why we watch so many sit-coms on television, and why we go to the theater to see Eddie Murphy films, and why comedians like Bob Hope, Carol Burnett, and Lucille Ball have been in such demand over the years. Laughter is the universal language of humankind. No matter where we go in the world, we hear laughter and we know, regardless of the differences in the spoken word, people are enjoying themselves.

People in troubled relationships usually find it difficult to laugh, especially at themselves. This is understandable, for they are too immersed in their pain to see the lighter side of things. For them, seriousness is the order of the day, and they are convinced that anxiety, depression, and helplessness are the kinds of feelings one should be experiencing at such a time. To even consider the possibility that there might be a bit of humor hidden within their predicament is, in their judgment, absurd.

This is why I find humor a very effective therapeutic intervention (if used wisely) in my counseling sessions from time to time. If I can reframe even a small chunk of the problem in a humorous vein, I find in many instances that the client begins to relax more, feels a sudden surge of hope, and allows herself or himself to play with the thought that perhaps all is not lost.

One of the biggest obstacles to effective marriage counseling is that by the time a couple arrives at the therapist's office, so much bad water has gone over the dam and both spouses are pretty much of a mind that very little, if anything, can be done to help them. They are discouraged over their failure to resolve their difficulties on their own. They are disappointed in themselves, confused, and quite dispirited. The last thing they would think of is the possibility that some of their behavior might be absurd, ridiculous, and even preposterous...and therefore honestly laughable! A hearty laugh can really clear away the fog of despair in a hurry.

That is where some counselors make a strategic mistake in their therapy. They are taught to establish rapport with a client by (among other tactics) mirroring, matching, and pacing the client's body movements, voice tone, facial expressions, gestures, etc. All this does work to gain rapport. However, once having rapport, if a counselor continues to mirror, match, and pace a client who is in "down-time" (depression, discouragement, despair, etc.), instead of attempting to intervene and lead the client to a less stressful emotional state, the whole session will be in down-time and no upward movement will take place. In fact, if this is done frequently enough, the counselor will become depressed! For my own sake, as well as for the good of the client, I use humor to make the intervention and precipitate the healing process, and at the same time, keep myself from really slipping into down-time.

Placing the wastebasket at the feet of the crying woman and pushing the tissue box closer to her is an example of what I mean. This little bit of humorous intervention was just enough to help her switch from tears to laughter to problem solving, the principal reason she had come to me in the first place.

Cathecting, in the form of crying, can be very therapeutic in itself; but at some point the effort to resolve the problem must commence, and the tears must be turned off so one can more clearly see the road ahead.

Recently, I met the most serious man in the whole world, possibly the most serious person ever! He could not accept the absurdity of life and enjoy it. He was a man addicted to the pursuit of life's meaning. Everything he encountered had to make sense to him; everything he experienced had to fit neatly into *his* rational conception of the world, or it was rejected. No one could remember the last time he laughed (nor could he) and barely could his wife recall the last time he smiled.

Needless to say, the atmosphere in the home was heavy, and even when he was not present, the family members continually caught themselves behaving as if they were attending a wake. And that is a fairly good description of how I felt when the family came in for counseling the first time. Try as I did,

way to go! She retorted that she was so paranoid at this point that even Mickey Mouse was suspect!

Laughter is such a wonderful detergent. It can clean up so many interpersonal conflicts so quickly. It can penetrate and dissolve so many petty disagreements and differences in half the time regular problem solving takes.

When we were growing up my grandmother used to caution us: "Never marry a person with no sense of humor. If you do, you'll probably spend the rest of your life trying to make them laugh." Of course, Grandmother assumed everyone should have a sense of humor, regardless of their background. She could not tolerate what she called "mopers," especially us kids when, in her opinion, we prolonged our funky blue periods. She would try to cheer us up and, if a smile was not forthcoming in the time she thought it should, then we were told to go off and sulk alone—Grandmother's variation on the theme, "Laugh and the world laughs with you. Cry and you cry alone!"

I vividly remember a time when I was a youngster and my happiness level was at an all-time low. My older sister had been invited to the seashore for the weekend, and I had not been allowed to go. I refused to be comforted and saw nothing humorous or enjoyable in my grandmother's efforts to cheer me up. For the better part of the morning of my sister's departure, I moped around, sulking and pouting my heart out. Finally my grandmother confronted me. Would I like to give up the tragedy, and go with her and my younger brother to the matinee, or stay at home and continue to bemoan my fate and the terrible injustices life deals out, especially to children who try so hard to be good. I opted for the tragedy and remained at home with my aunt, who was so caught up in her boyfriend, she hardly noticed me.

As I recall, I spent a very lonely afternoon in my room, desperately struggling to maintain my position of social reject. I kept envisioning how my family would come together in the early evening, find me missing, then search and discover me huddled in one corner of my bedroom, barely able to move from lack of nourishment (no lunch or snacks), quietly weeping as I agonized over my fate.

Around three o'clock, I was utterly bored of the whole scenario and went downstairs just in time to greet my grandmother and brother returning from what they agreed was one of the best Disney movies they had ever seen...and the popcorn had been particularly warm, salty, and buttery!

I am convinced that incident was the beginning of my serious learning about how to laugh some things off and get on with living. After all, where did my moping get me? I lost out on two counts; not only was I denied the opportunity of going to the shore, but I foolishly denied myself the other opportunity of going to the movies.

Couples in troubled relationships often demonstrate attitudes and behaviors similar to the childlike attitudes and behavior I demonstrated. Rather than look for the humor in a conflictual episode, they pout, sulk, and mope. More often than not, they end up losing on both ends simply because they could not overcome their negative thinking and laugh it off.

Randy and Glenn are slowly losing each other. Rarely are they able to let go of an unpleasant situation between them and laugh it off. Randy tends to magnify a problem, and Glenn tends to personalize everything. How is that for a combination!

When Glenn was passed over for a promotion in his company, Randy decided it was the end of the world, and Glenn was convinced his wife was blaming him for his loss of additional income and prestige. There was no consoling Randy on that occasion. She just knew Glenn was washed up at the corporation and would soon be replaced by a younger junior executive. Then what would they do? At his age, how could he ever get another comparable position with another company? All was lost, as far as she was concerned.

Of course, Randy had no shred of evidence to support her projections, and that is largely why her husband, who usually took adverse criticism personally, felt she was criticizing him quite severely. Unfortunately, Glenn was also criticizing himself rather severely. He also had a need to be a shining light in his professional life, a superstar of sorts in the business world. So, deep within he was holding court, and the final verdict was guilty. He had failed his family as well as himself...or had he?

Unaware, at first, of what was happening, Randy and Glenn began to separate, psychologically, each engrossed in his and her own little world of painful disappointment and confusion. Life became very serious, and laughter a stranger. Even when Glenn was appointed to a corporate division planning committee, Randy was unimpressed. She minimized the positive aspects of his promotion by declaring it was J.B.'s way of patting Glenn on the head and pacifying him. Glenn was certain it was meant to be a vote of confidence...but then he wasn't so sure of that either. So they argued more, and they sometimes even fought!

By the time they were referred to me, they had pretty much concluded their marriage was over. The corporate monster had devastated their relationship. They could hardly see eye-to-eye on anything. I suggested they had been jumping to conclusions, probably for some time. I then went on to suggest they might have taken a partly negative situation and made it a catastrophe that sorely influenced their thinking from that point on. People like Randy and Glenn have a penchant for doing that. Glenn did hesitatingly admit my hypothesis might be correct, whereas Randy refused to even consider the possibility. It was apparent both were inundated with negative thinking at that point in their relationship.

How different were Wally and Merti when faced with a similar situation. Wally was a partially disabled Vietnam veteran who could only hold down a part-time job. He became Mr. Homemaker while Merti pursued her business career. She, too, was passed over for a promotion that would have meant a substantial increase in salary and benefits, something she and Wally were confidently expecting. Corporate politics, however, decreed otherwise, and Merti stayed where she was with all indications pointing to the strong possibility she had reached her ceiling with the company.

Naturally they were bitterly disappointed, and reacted with appropriate anger and fear. Soon, however, they realized they were slipping into a negative pattern of thinking, which was influencing their feelings and behavior. They decided to sit themselves down and try to reframe the entire situation.

"Reframing" is a term used to describe the mental or internal act of looking at a situation from various perspectives just as you might view a painting differently each time you place it in a different frame.

Some people can more easily reframe situations or events than others can. Wally and Merti, for example, were able to reframe their situation much more quickly and effectively than were Randy and Glenn. In fact, the latter couple never actually did evaluate Glenn's failure to be promoted from any perspective other than just that: a big failure! They were never able or willing to recognize the flip side of the situation as the other couple did. Wally and Merti decided it really was all for the best. After all, a promotion for Merti would have meant more time away from home and more stress on the job, two things neither of them really wanted. In discussing the matter, they even found themselves laughing over the way Merti described her boss's feeble stammering and stuttering attempts to soften the blow when he called her into his office. She was certain he was scared to death she would counter-attack by drumming up charges of sexual harassment against him!

Reframing with humor is a wonderful way to enjoy some of the absurdity and ridiculousness found in so many negative situations. Quality marriage couples reframe with humor and see the lighter side of things when faced with distressful happenings in their lives. They can laugh it off and take life a little less seriously. A certain optimism surrounds them, and even though they may get down at times, they rarely stay down.

I have found quality marriage couples to be more multi-ordinal in their thinking processes than uni-ordinal. Multi-ordinal thinkers examine and evaluate something from many perspectives before drawing conclusions or making decisions. They are able to see both sides of something. Uni-ordinal thinkers, on the other hand, are examiners and evaluators. They can see both sides of something, but *only* both sides, one of which is correct or mostly correct, and the other is incorrect or mostly incorrect. It is either this or that, but it can't be both at the same time; it is pretty much the way they surmise reality.

They are dichotomous in their reasoning and may at times portray the Archie Bunker approach in evaluating a situation.[2]

The uni-ordinal person, for example, decides that something is humorous or seriously painful. He finds it difficult to evaluate some event, for instance, as being humorous in part and also seriously painful. For him, it has to be one or the other. For the multi-ordinal person, however, even death has its humor, e.g., the traditional Irish wake. The multi-ordinal thinkers can laugh, cry, be serious, and react intelligently and effectively, all at the same time.

Here is an interesting twist. Uni-ordinal people sometimes think multi-ordinally, and vice versa. A great deal depends upon the specific circumstances. I know a fellow who is rather renowned for his multi-ordinal thinking powers at work; but at home, in relation to his three teenage daughters, he is quite uni-ordinal...at least as far as they are concerned. They constantly complain that their dad sees only his own side of an issue and will not even consider what they think.

If you think that being more consistently multi-ordinal is better than being uni-ordinal, you are being uni-ordinal in your thinking! You are also thinking correctly! Multi-ordinal couples have more fun, for one thing. Their creative juices flow more readily because their imaginations receive greater stimulation from the variety of ways they view a situation. It must be cautioned, however, that a uni-ordinal response is more appropriate in many, many situations in life—humor or no humor notwithstanding. If the shark is several feet away and you are inches from the rope ladder that will bring you out of the water to safety, you had better be thinking in an uni-ordinal manner. You can get multi-ordinal over a Miller Lite later on.

On the whole, however, people in quality relationships generally react to negative situations in a multi-ordinal fashion, which allows them frequently to find some humor in their plight, and thus reduce or even eliminate the emotional pain they initially experience. How do they do this? They talk to themselves, they talk to each other, and they talk to friends who are good listeners.

We all talk to ourselves. That is one of the ways we think. We carry on conversations in our heads and make evaluations and decisions based upon our conclusions. The only time talking to oneself may be a symptom of mental or emotional disturbance is if we actually believe that in carrying on a conversation within ourselves, we are actually speaking with someone else!

Take Audry and Noel, for example. Some people could not understand how resigned and apparently cheerful they appeared shortly after their only child, a nine-year-old son, died of leukemia. Some individuals were convinced they were still in shock, and did not yet fully realize the impact of their loss. Not so. Each had gone inside for many isolated hours and mentally and emotionally talked out the excruciating experience. Each, in her and his own being, felt the anger, the grief, the pain of loss, and finally the acceptance and resignation.

They talked to each other and to their intimate and trusted friends as they tried desperately to understand and accept their fate. In so doing, they became multi-ordinal in their thinking; as they talked internally and externally, they began to *see* their son's death from different perspectives (reframing). A few skeptics and pessimists called it rationalization, especially when Audry voiced the feeling that she felt good about her son being with his grandfather (her deceased father) in heaven and not having to go through all the heartaches of this life. These same people were somewhat horrified when Audry and Noel attended the Saint Patrick's Dance three weeks after the burial and had a good time!

Noel explained their behavior. He said that after all is said and done he and his wife firmly believe that their beloved son had died, would never return to them no matter how many tears were shed, and was forever happy in heaven; and that he and Audry ought to get on with their lives and enjoy themselves as best they can while they could, because their little son had shown them how short life really is. And so they had a genuinely good time at the parish Saint Patrick's Dance.

*Footnote*: To this day, they both thank God they were able to talk about it and see different perspectives! They eventually found themselves laughing over some of the humorous moments they had had with their little one.

It feels good to laugh.

## CHAPTER FIVE

# Erasers Are for Lesser Gods

"Blessed are those who suffer *not* from psychic constipation, for they are better able to grow satisfying and lasting marriages."

Some people are much more able to forgive and forget than others. Adrienne, unfortunately, is not one of them. She came to the first counseling session loaded for bear. She had a steel trap memory and could recall with the precision of a diamond cutter every *faux pas* Alex ever committed during their seven shaky years of marriage. Alex, on the other hand, can't even recall what he had for dinner the previous night.

Adrienne suffers from a chronic case of psychic constipation. She cannot let go of past events, so much so that she spends much of her time and energy dwelling on the past, which affords her little contact with the present. Even that wouldn't be so ludicrous were it not for the fact that all her brooding is negative and ultimately self-defeating.

Recently something else has been occurring. She has taken to reciting her husband's litany of faults and failings in the presence of others. Alex tries to make light of it, but his patience is wearing thin these days.

I recommend this sort of nonsense if you are really not interested in a quality relationship. Dwelling on your partner's goofs, mistakes, and failures, along with the obnoxious habit of airing your dirty laundry in public, especially in the presence of relatives or business associates, can be, and usually is, disastrous to a relationship. Growing a quality marriage requires a couple to practice compassion and loyalty toward each other. These virtues go hand-in-glove; you can't have one without the other.

Trudy and Bob possess these virtues and demonstrate them in a most admirable way. Only rarely does either one suffer from psychic constipation and begin to mind dwell. And neither can be cited for serious violations of loyalty. As a matter of fact, they are known by relatives and friends as very confidential people.

What is their secret? Well, Bob was raised in a compassionate family. As he says, "We were also taught to keep our dirty laundry in the basement." Trudy was not as fortunate. She readily admits her family environment was anything but compassionate and loyal. Her father was forever reminding everyone in the family of their past errors and letting all the neighborhood know about them, too. It was contagious because Trudy, her mother, and two brothers gradually developed psychic constipation, and then the whole family learned to dwell on the past, cast blame, and air each other's foibles and faults.

Bob and his family were a great help to Trudy when they were courting. Their example of compassion and loyalty toward each family member, toward others, and especially toward Trudy as she struggled to de-condition herself in this matter enabled her eventually to enter marriage with the strong resolution to practice compassion and loyalty in her own marriage and family life.

To err is human. To forgive is...really tough at times! Compassion is the virtue that enables you to forgive, especially when it is really difficult to do. The compassionate person, such as my wife Kate, accepts the fallibility of human nature. She realizes that to be humanly perfect is one thing; to be perfectly human is yet another!

A play on words? Not so. To be humanly perfect may be a noble goal, but it is absurd to think you can actually attain perfection in this life. To be perfectly human, however, is to be exactly what you are, human, and therefore subject to imperfections! To be human means to be imperfect: to make mistakes and fail on occasion. The compassionate person understands and accepts this, first in regard to self, and then with regard to others.

This is terribly important to remember: You can only show compassion toward others if you can show compassion toward yourself. Kate can forgive herself. That is why she can forgive others so readily. In response to my inquiry as to how she could be so forgiving, to herself and others, she said that as an elementary school creative writing teacher, she had long ago come to appreciate erasers. She always had her pupils draft their new stories in pencil first. That way, when they made a mistake, she could address the mistake and help the child learn from it. Then the pupil could instantly rub out the error, make it disappear, and act as though it had never happened, then happily get on with the story, which is what drafting a piece of writing is all about. She insisted that her "little ones" never get hung up on their errors, but that they move on toward the completion of their writings.

That's how Kate feels about life. It is ridiculous to harbor guilt over your own *faux pas* or to feel resentment and disappointment over the failings of others *ad nauseam*. "If you can't get on with life and you are unwilling to forgive and erase whatever happened, you're stuck," she asserts. She once summed up her thoughts on the matter quite succinctly when she said, "As far as I'm concerned, erasers are for us lesser gods, and I need to use as big an eraser as I can find!"

Kate came to our marriage equipped with a very big eraser, indeed. And for sixteen years she has been using it quite readily on herself, on me, and on others. I'm not trying to say, however, that my wife is a walkin', talkin' saint! She has her moments when she has to struggle with psychic constipation, but it never seems to be for long. I call her the overnight forgiver, perhaps I should say, "forgetter." How many times in our married life I'd wake in the morning feeling the heaviness of remorse still lingering from the previous evening's conflict only to discover that she had to be reminded of it in some detail. She had forgotten about it!

There have been times when "the sun has gone down on our anger" at each other, but more often than not, with the dawn has come forgiveness and forgetting. Much of that is due to Kate. I've learned from her example.

I've also learned something else, something I call "counting your similarities." It has helped me on many occasions when my gut reaction has been to strike out verbally, blame and condemn someone for a situation I found unacceptable and totally intolerable.

When we were newlyweds, I found Kate's failure to be on time for appointments exasperating and increasingly irritating, for it was a continual source of embarrassment to me. I tried to pretend it did not upset me, but this gunnysacking approach did not last very long.

One evening when I was pacing the floor, anxiously waiting for her to make her final departure from the bathroom, I could not restrain myself any longer. I exploded, knowing full well that a donnybrook loomed on the horizon. I did not care. We were already forty minutes late for the dinner party, and I had had it with her insensitivity toward me and the friends who invited us.

I was correct. The donnybrook took place. It was short-lived, but poignant for both of us. At least two significant results came out of it: We ended up an hour late for the party, and the other was much more positive in the long run. Somehow or other in the heat of the dispute, I managed to hear something Kate said that I hadn't heard before and certainly hadn't considered. In response to my accusing posture, she retorted that she too felt exasperated, irritated, and downright embarrassed whenever people dropped by unexpectedly and I nonverbally showed my disapproval that they had not called first.

What we had going was a double values collision. On the one hand, I put great stock into being on time for scheduled occasions and wanting people to call before just popping in on us. On the other hand, Kate put equal stock into making sure everything was in proper order, including herself, before leaving the house for any function (which usually was the cause for most of our tardiness), and in wanting people to feel free to drop in anytime for a visit.

I heard what she said, but I was not willing at the moment to consider her comparison, so I did what any normal human being would likely do in the heat of battle. I threw her a "yes-but-and" hooker: "*Yes*, it's true I get bent out of shape when friends just pop in as though we had nothing better to do than sit around waiting for them. *But* I feel quite justified because their sudden appearance at the front door makes our two watchdogs go bananas and practically destroy the window sill with their nails. *And* besides, there is a big difference between wanting people to call first and making people wait upon our late arrival *all* the time."

Since Kate was also being a normal human being, she naturally counter-responded with her "yes-but-and" hooker: "*Yes*, I know we are late sometimes, and sometimes it's my fault. *But* I told you I'm a poor judge of time; all our friends know it, so they don't get their knees in a knot. I don't know what you are so worried about. *And* besides, more than one person has told me how uncomfortable they feel when they stop by and you are home. So don't talk to me about insensitivity!"

With this hooker we quickly moved into a familiar round-about position, something that usually occurs in a values collision when spouses become overly defensive. They go around in circles, each upholding their own perspective on the matter at hand, and more often than not, dredging up past examples of the other's inappropriate behavior in support of their own position.

We did a round-about until we reached our friends' home, then gave it up. Fortunately, we both enjoy a good party, so it wasn't too great a sacrifice to abandon the argument and lose ourselves in the good drinks, tasty food, and interesting conversation.

On the way home, we were able to discuss the incident in a

more mellow manner and arrived at the mutually acceptable conclusion that although the circumstances were somewhat different in each case, our behavior was similar. Neither one considered the other's value system! Neither one considered the other's feelings! Simply because of the specific context each of us favored—I was justified in my anger because people should not be late for appointments and Kate was justified in her anger because people should feel free to drop by the house anytime— each felt that it made the difference, and therefore made one of us *right* and the other *wrong!*

Incidentally, this is what arguing is all about. I decide my position (context, values, and feelings) is right and yours is wrong, since it differs from mine. Now I proceed to bombard you with all the rational and emotive reasons I can think of to support my position and shoot down yours. Naturally, unless you are a bona-fide Caspar Milquetoast, you will do the same. Of course, there are variations on the theme, but the run-of-the-mill argument, especially between married partners, is pretty much the way I just described it; in effect, they become sparring partners.

Scripture cautions us: "You who are without sin cast the first stone." Counting your similarities is somewhat the same thing. The bit of insight Kate and I gleaned from this experience led us to devise a strategy for siphoning off some of the anger and irritation we feel when one or the other of us ignores a value the other holds dear. "Counting your similarities" is how we tag this strategy.

Before confronting your husband or wife, stop to think of some behavior you indulge in that causes similar grief to your partner. What is the reason for this chunk of mental gymnastics? If you are really being honest with yourself (no yes-but game), the awareness of the similarity in behavior can help quiet the negative feelings and allow a more rational approach to the issue at hand.

Take Eli for example. She and Ryan have been married for twelve years, with a quality relationship going. One reason is that they have learned the counting-your-similarities strategy over the years. No one actually taught them this strategy;

they stumbled upon it in somewhat the same manner as Kate and myself. Eli loves to tell the story.

She is ready to admit that she is sort of a neurotic when it comes to keeping house. Everything has its place, and only when everything is in its place does Eli feel she can relax. As fate would have it, she fell in love and married a man who pretty much cared less about how the house looked, so long as he and Eli were getting along, the children were healthy and happy, and there was plenty of beer in the refrigerator.

One thing that continually irritated Eli and led to many useless arguments early in their marriage was Ryan's apparent disregard for Eli's need to have everything in the house in perfect order, especially when her parents came to visit. Invariably she would "break her neck," as she put it, to have the house and children in top-notch order, spic and span, in anticipation of her parents' arrival, only to find her neatnik efforts quickly sabotaged by the careless antics of her thoughtless but well-meaning husband: the morning newspaper left on the family room floor, shoes kicked off and abandoned in the hallway, soiled clothing piled beside the clothes hamper, the peanut butter jar, opened loaf of bread, and sticky knife bunched together in the middle of the kitchen table.

Her repeated reprimands were getting her nowhere fast. It wasn't that Ryan was deliberately being stubborn or obstinate in the face of his wife's accusations. It was simply that from his own upbringing he was conditioned otherwise and saw no harm in "living normal," as he put it. He'd make efforts to change, but they never lasted very long.

Then one day during one of their more heated arguments, Eli finally heard Ryan say something that he had often said before. This time, for some reason, it struck and stuck, enough that Eli went off, thought quite a bit about it, and began to make some changes in her own behavior.

What was it her husband said? He reminded her that no matter how many times he had asked her not to forget to record the checks she writes and balance their checkbook when using it, she still failed to do so on most occasions, causing any number of checks to bounce as a result. "When it comes to money, Eli," he said, "you are an extremely careless and untidy woman! You are thoughtless and evidently uncaring about the penalties we have to pay and the consequent loss of income! As far as I can see, in this matter you are everything you claim I am."

When Eli tells the story she says that she had heard Ryan say these things before, but this time it really hit home, and she found herself beginning to admit he was correct in his observation. She was as untidy in their financial bookkeeping matters as he was around the house.

As they later talked about this, they became more and more aware of other areas of their lives where they objected to the other's behavior; yet through further and honest reflection they realized they were similar. What did all this do in the final analysis? It helped them become more compassionate toward each other, and more accepting of each other's faults and failings. They didn't stop arguing, but their spats became less frequent and much less painful.

It is no easy task to stop and count your similarities. Many times, it is easier to pretend you are without sin and go ahead and cast the first stone. That is because counting your similarities requires a good deal of internal work. Ask Eli. Ask me or Kate. Ask anyone who struggles honestly to come to terms with his or her own human condition.

Eli says she initially wanted so badly to deny there was any similarity between her poorly managed checkbook and her husband's lack of tidiness around the house. I felt the same way in regard to my conflict with Kate over her persistent lateness and my continual resistance to people just dropping by the house. I played the yes-but-and game so long before I finally acknowledged that Kate had as much of a case as I did, and her anger and embarrassment were just as real (valid) as mine.

Eli recalls that she had begun to lay awake at night and picture in her mind's eye the unbalanced checkbook with all the entry gaps and crossed out estimated entries, and the time that Ryan spent at the desk trying to reconcile the inconsistencies, and the horrible reactions he had when the overdraft statements came in the mail. And she heard herself explaining to him that she didn't take the time to record the expenditures because she did not want to keep people waiting in the checkout line at the supermarket, or forgetting to write in the amount because she was too busy trying to keep the children in line.

She also began to hear Ryan explaining why he would forget to pick up the newspaper and put it in the garage after reading it, or why he never remembered to put his socks in the hamper not in a ball, or why he persisted in leaving things around, and closet doors ajar, drawers partly open, and whatever.

Funny thing. She began to understand—not accept, but understand. And that made it easier to tolerate; at least it wasn't that big a deal! She still tries at times to persuade him to pick up after himself. Sometimes he does, sometimes he doesn't. And even when they argue about it, it's no longer the end of the world. She remembers the checkbook!

Have you ever noticed how often people are so compassionate toward others, but have little or no compassion for their loved ones. Ironic, isn't it? I suppose there are any number of reasons for this sad situation. One that is of prime consideration is the matter of marital expectations.

Any marital counselor will tell you that in every problematic situation between husband and wife, there is always the issue of expectations involved, regardless of whatever else is present to the conflict. I can't begin to count the times I have listened to disconsolate spouses voice their disappointment, dissatisfaction, and heartache over the failure of their partners to live up to their expectations in some fashion or other.

Let's face it. It's much easier to be compassionate toward someone when we have little or no expectations of them, or when their failure or mistake has little or no direct impact on our lives. We expect much more from those with whom we have an intimate relationship. Our expectations can quickly turn into marital demands unless we are careful to distinguish between the two.

People enjoying quality marriages do indeed distinguish between marital expectations and demands. And it's a great deal

more than simply a question of terminology. It's a matter of belief, attitude, and consequent behavior. That is why they are
compassionate toward each other. People whose relationships
are in trouble invariably confuse expectations and demands.
People in satisfying and lasting relationships do not. What's
the difference?

An expectation is the mental projection of some event into the
future. It may be the immediate future, it may be the more dis-
tant future, but it's the future, not the past or present. Ellen
stands at the altar, her husband-to-be at her side. As the mini-
ster prays over them, she mentally steps out of the present and
projects herself into the future, picturing herself and her husband moving out of their apartment and into a new home within
the year. That's a visual (and emotional) expectation, something she is looking forward to; she sees herself doing it, perhaps imagining herself hanging a picture on the living room
wall or making the new four-poster bed for the first time or
helping to move the sofa closer to the fireplace.

Earl is also standing at the altar with Ellen, his bride, at
his side. He, too, mentally leaves the present for the moment
and projects into the near future, thinking about how their combined incomes will allow them to invest in the boss's real estate
enterprise before they begin to have a family. He sees himself
talking with his boss and hears himself making risky, yet sensible, suggestions regarding the financial growth of the company. He, too, was enjoying an expectation.

Two people, each with an expectation, but what a difference
between their expectations. And neither expectation was ful-
filled. Within six months after they returned from their honeymoon, Ellen's husband lost his sales position because he repeatedly missed his cold call sales quota. That meant the move
to purchase a house was put on ice until he could secure another
position with at least an equal income.

Ellen was terribly disappointed and heartbroken. She was
also very compassionate toward her husband. She didn't like
what happened one bit, no more than he did, but she did not
blame, condemn, or accuse him, even when she discovered that

his increasingly frequent trips to the Atlantic City casinos had a great deal to do with his poor sales record of late. She was compassionate, and she was also resolute in her determination to lick this potentially fatal problem before it destroyed their marriage.

Actually, Ellen had two expectations that were challenged early in her marriage. One was the fantasy of a home of her own soon after marriage, and the other was that her husband was and would always be a stable, hard-working individual with no skeletons in the closet.

Her compassion paid off. Her husband responded to her understanding and patience. They have their home. He has become quite a supersalesman in recent years, and occasionally they drop into Atlantic City for some fun.

Bill's one expectation (he had many!) of accumulating enough income to invest substantially in the real estate market was also unfulfilled. Kathy decided shortly after they were married to become pregnant and start a family before she got too old to enjoy her child. Of course, this tore Bill's long-range financial plans to shreds. He was beside himself with anger, resentment, fear. As far as he was concerned, his wife had betrayed him by changing her mind, and there was no way he would permit her to get pregnant. A few years hence, yes, but not now!

No matter how hard she tried to explain to him why she had a change of heart and what it would mean to both of them (from her perspective) to become parents, he would not budge. He demanded that she continue on the pill, and he wanted to hear no more about it! Either she abide by their previous agreement or the marriage was all over! Kathy agreed. She readily admitted she had honestly agreed to this arrangement before their wedding. So she continued to work until their divorce about two years later.

When expectations become cast in concrete they become marital demands. Bill's expectation was really a demand; there was no leverage or flexibility built in. "Either it happens, and happens the way I expect it to, or I don't play!" There is no room for compassion when an expectation becomes a demand. There is no latitude, no space, no room for negotiations or even compromise. This stringent, demanding attitude may be most appropriate for a military leader in a combat zone, but it doesn't work very well in a marital relationship that naturally requires a good deal of compassionate interaction.

Quality marriages involve husbands and wives who entertain few expectations of each other and even less demands. This is so because these men and women were initially attracted to their spouses and came to appreciate them for what they were at the time, not for what they expected them to develop into. And what expectations they did have were appropriately derived through considerations of the past, present, and future in order to prevent disappointment later on.

Conjugal loyalty is the companion virtue to conjugal compassion. A person who is truly compassionate is also an equally loyal person. Loyalty has to do with privacy and confidentiality and that means, as Bob put it, "keeping the dirty laundry in the basement."

I still remember how uncomfortable I was at a New Year's Eve party several years ago when the hostess launched into a tirade about her husband's emotional dependency upon his mother. I can picture his face yet, crimson with humiliation and anger. He could have killed her on the spot. The majority of the party guests were his working staff and their partners.

Granted, she may have been completely frustrated with her husband's relationship with his mother, but a social gathering of people who looked up to her husband as a competent manager was hardly the time to ventilate her helplessness. Unfortunately, this was a rather routine occurrence, as I later learned. More unfortunately, she apparently never saw her catharsis as a breach of loyalty to him.

This was an extreme case. Telling tales out of school goes on rather regularly; most of it is done without conscious malice, I will admit. It is supposedly done in a spirit of fun and normal conversation (whatever that means!), but the covert effects in the long run are often devastating to a person's character and to the marriage relationship.

People who have marital relationship problems need someone in whom they can confide, and seek support and advice. I don't deny that. Thank God, we have empathic parents, aunts, uncles, and friends who can listen and console without making your problem a community issue. Thank goodness, we have professionals who are trained to guide and counsel you when needed.

What a married couple does not need is a "band of siders," as I call them, who are only too willing to listen to your plight, rejoice in the fact that you are as bad off as they are, and are happily willing to give you advice that hasn't worked for them. There are also those who really don't know what to say in response to your litany of complaints, feel very uncomfortable as you expound on your woes, and wish they had never met you! In this case, you are not only doing yourself and your spouse a grave disservice, but you are placing your audience in a unenviable position.

Many things said in jest about one's spouse are the fuel that feeds the fires of resentment, disappointment, disgust, and finally disintegration of the relationship. "I only meant it as a joke" is a line that frequently signals the beginning of the end. The lasting and satisfying marriages I am familiar with are being grown by men and women who can occasionally joke about their spouse's foibles, but know well where to draw the line.

## CHAPTER SIX

# In Praise of Time-Outs

Couples enjoying quality marriages know well the value of taking time out. They recognize that as satisfying and rewarding as their relationships may be, unless they make room for "R and R," the stresses of life will gradually take their toll on even the healthiest of conjugal unions.

We hear and read a great deal these days about stress and its debilitating effects. Since approximately 75 percent of all of today's illness is traced to stress, and some estimates of the incidence of stress-related illnesses run as high as 90 percent, it is no wonder that people are suddenly quite interested in stress management. Such interest is not confined to the managers of business and industry by any means. Counselors and therapists are seeing more and more husbands and wives whose relationships are adversely affected because of various stress factors, and they are reaching out for help in managing these factors.

What are these stress factors? Actually, anything that proves harmful to one's physical and mental well-being. Stress is a fact of life, and some stress is positive and motivating. Too much stress, however, becomes debilitating to both mind and body, causing psychological and physiological disturbances such as anxiety, tension, depression, confusion, increased use of alcohol and drugs, insomnia, headaches, hypertension, ulcers, colitis, asthma, peripheral vascular disease, angina, increased blood pressure, heart attacks, and strokes.

The more common sources of stress (stress factors) in the marital context are: job pressures (meeting deadlines, too much or too little work, interpersonal conflicts with superiors or fellow workers), all of which can spill over into the home life and familial relationships, causing discord and conflict; personal life pressures (sickness, death of a loved one, sexual and/or financial problems, two-career couple, in-laws, children); environmental pressures (noise levels, overcrowding, weather, physical safety).

From this abbreviated list of stress factors, it is easy to see that pressure and demands on our energy and time come from every corner of our lives and can contribute very poignantly to marital strife and disharmony, unless we do something about it. And people in quality relationships do something about it. That is why they enjoy satisfying and lasting marriages.

What do they do? Some couples actually design stress-control programs that involve rather sophisticated and regimented types of stress-reduction strategies. Other couples engage in more simplified and spontaneous sorts of stress-management techniques.

Ferris and Kelly belong to the first classification. They take pride in their program of stress control and well-being which, when clearly explained, is a fine example of the preventive medicine approach to stress and the promotion of health. They and their children are strong advocates of regular exercise, for instance. They are convinced that it is a very effective way to prevent or relieve physical and mental tension. They believe that during exercise, tranquilizing chemicals called endorphins are released in the brain, bringing pleasurable relaxation. They are quite religious about exercising; they might walk, swim, jog, or bicycle at least thirty minutes, four to five times a week.

An interesting sidelight is that when Ferris is on the road traveling up and down the East Coast, that doesn't stop him from exercising. Before meeting his clients for breakfast, he jogs four miles around the hotel parking area and uses the stairs rather than an elevator, when possible. His associates are convinced he is addicted. He is, and that is fine with him; at least, as he claims, it's a positive addiction.

Every member of the family also has a hobby; it's part of their program. Kelly is very much into needlepoint and Ferris loves to garden. The children, of course, are deeply involved in various school- and church-related projects. The point is, whatever hobby or hobbies they have chosen provides a creative outlet that helps to lessen fatigue and refresh them physically and psychologically.

Ferris and Kelly are quite adamant about the eat right and feel right portion of their program and they have done a good job of convincing their children to reduce their intake of sugar, sodium, fatty foods, junk food, etc. Friends and neighbors kid them about their obsession with their stress control and wellness program, but they don't mind. They've noticed lately that some of their "kidders" are beginning to walk and jog!

Other couples take time out in less regimented ways, the informal approach to stress control. Marian does not follow a fixed schedule of physical exercise, nor does her husband Rex. When they feel uptight, however, they make it a point to drag out the bicycles and peddle away their tensions. Both insist on getting enough sleep during weeknights at least to insure their effectiveness at the office. They feel they are tuned into their stress thresholds and sensibly respond to any overload they may begin to feel.

When working with married couples at seminars as well as in private practice, I am occasionally asked what I think about spouses taking separate time-outs. I like that question because it gives me the opportunity to address several issues related to that one item.

First of all, I am in favor of married couples getting away from the ordinary, everyday routine of life, including their children, and going off together for a shared time-out, however short or long it may be. I'm also in favor of this sort of mini-sabbatical several times a year.

When I make this statement, I usually get some friendly flack from a few who think it takes a bundle of dollars to enjoy a time-out. My answer is always the same: Time-outs don't have to take place in far-off, expensive places. If you can afford that kind of trip, do it. Time-outs come packaged in any number of sizes and prices. I know a couple who retreat to a lovely little motel for a weekend from time to time. The motel is five miles from their house!

Couples in quality marriages, make no mistake, take time out as often as they can reasonably afford it, be it for a day, a weekend, a week, whatever. In their own way they "go apart and rest awhile," heeding the advice of the gospel. Growing satisfying and lasting relationships demands the periodic time-out. One intimate really gets to know the other more in the midst of relaxation than in everyday living.

Married partners who find any and every excuse not to take a time-out, and those who seemingly take delight in feeling the pressure and stresses of family life and work, are asking for trouble. They would have you believe they would love to get away, but the press of work, or the children, or the finances, or something else deprives them of the opportunity.

Workaholics are especially annoying when they speak as if they were indispensable to their jobs and cannot possibly find the time to play a bit. I'm unimpressed. There is no doubt that those husbands and wives who take time out to rest, relax, and play together stay together.

As for the question of whether or not separate time-outs in the form of vacations is advisable, my answer is a definite yes/no, i.e., there are conditions attached. One, that both partners agree to the arrangement. Two, that the separate time-out is not an excuse for freelance loving, etc. Three, that the length of time away from each other is mutually acceptable. And four, that the frequency of separate time-outs is mutually acceptable.

And a fifth condition, that there are also shared time-outs

the relationship. I know of a couple (long since divorced) who always took separate time-outs, never together. This was at the husband's insistence. The wife complied for years, then finally decided to take a time-out for herself...permanently.

A young couple in counseling, married two and a half years, are having a severe problem with time-outs. It is somewhat complicated in that the husband not only insists upon his right to continue his prenuptial routine of taking a week off in the late fall for deer hunting with the club and one in the spring for deep-sea fishing (with the club), but also demands his young bride get off his back about his Wednesday and Friday nights' weekly tavern and card-playing ritual. How long do you think this one will last unless some changes are made?

The young man's reasoning goes something like this: "I may be married, but I'm also an individual. I work hard (which he does) and need the time off away from her to be with my friends and let my hair down. I have a *right* to this, and she *ought* to understand why I feel this way. I have no problem with her visiting her family in Utah or going out with her girl friends once in a while."

What about the young wife? She is ready to pack it in. Her idea of us-ness obviously contradicts her husband's. She finds herself sitting alone at home more and more or looking for distractions in her few female friendships. Sad to say, they are poles apart in their ideas of us-ness and time-outs...and much more!

This couple's situation is somewhat extreme, yet not altogether infrequent, and not simply among young married people either. She wants to do things together, he wants his space. He feels he is being smothered; she feels rejected, manipulated, and taken for granted. The more she nags, the stronger his case becomes: He needs to relieve the stress of living with her. The more he neglects the us-ness in the marriage, the more she is sure it was all a mistake.

This sounds like a can-this-marriage-be-saved scenario, doesn't it? Why bring it up? This kind of situation arises when time-outs are misunderstood and abused. Couples sincerely in love know better. They know that separate time-outs can help to keep partners from smothering each other (a prime cause of marital discontent), yet they are mature enough to know how and when to balance their separate time-outs. Can they offer us some advice on this?

Randy and Denise, married seven years with two children, handle their time-outs quite equitably. They use the "his," "hers," and "our" approach. Randy is into racquet ball on Wednesday nights, while Denise is a devotee of tennis on Thursday evenings. They both love card games, and twice a month they join their friends for a round of poker or bridge. They also love to wine, dine, and dance, so one night a month is usually spent enjoying such entertainment in various "searched out" spots in the city. If their budget does not allow this luxury at any given time, they substitute a quick bite to eat and a movie, or the theater...and dance at home.

Randy loves sports, especially football and ice hockey. That "addiction," as Denise refers to it, could have made for many long and lonely falls and winters for her except for the fact that he has learned to set priorities for his needs and wants in order to accommodate the relationship, which wasn't easy to do at first.

Denise is more of a warm weather sports person. She enjoys tennis and swimming and occasionally watching a baseball game. She couldn't care less about football or ice hockey. But she respects her husband's values, as he does hers, and for the most part they are able and willing to balance each other's preferences.

How? Denise says one thing they learned early in their marriage was to level with each other when they felt an injustice or felt neglected, used, or taken for granted. There was the time, for example, when Randy thought she was spending far too much time on the telephone each evening. Denise, of course, thought otherwise. She saw it as a pleasant time-out after a long day at work.

When Randy first told her about his feelings on the matter, Denise was fit to be tied and reminded him in no uncertain terms of the hours he spent in front of the TV watching his sacred sports events. They had a real blowout the first time around.

Once the smoke cleared, however, they got down to the business of "balancing their acts."

To this day they are convinced they were able and willing to work through their differences regarding time-outs because they were aware and committed to the us-ness in their marriage. Through their honesty with each other and their willingness to listen to each other, plus their desire to resolve their differences equitably (win-win), they successfully worked toward a compatible balance regarding their time-outs apart.

Randy speaks of the need to let go in such circumstances. He says that as they discussed the situation (over several months), they each became aware of the need to let go of their individual wants and began to control their lives in such a way that the relationship took precedence. What they happily discovered was that the more they let go in favor of us-ness, the more they felt like individuals. *They felt free to give...and receive.*

What they experienced is yet another key to a quality relationship. The more they each gave to the other, the more they each received from the other! Their separate time-outs apart became healthy outlets for managing their stress rather than becoming the source of accelerating their stress.

The time-outs that satisfying and lasting relationships use come in many sizes and shapes, many colors and fabrics. What appeals to one couple may be taboo to another. There is, however, a common denominator present in all quality marriages. Husbands and wives in such marriages are intelligently aware of unique stressful situations in their lives and take steps to reduce the stress load by finding and using a stress-reduction strategy specifically geared to their situation(s). I label it preventive medicine.

Couples often find themselves in trouble because they are not aware of situations that cause stress. For years Henrietta kept quiet about things her husband did that rubbed her the wrong way. She was a gunnysacker par excellence. After a severe bout with ulcers and a series of migraine headaches, she finally sought help in an effort to be more assertive and open. That is a good example of debilitating stress. For years she did not even recognize her physical ailments were directly related to the stress she imposed upon herself by her closed-mouth approach to her husband's unacceptable behaviors.

Another common denominator in quality relationships regarding stress management has to do with a mental attitude or mind-set about the fundamental cause of stress, regardless of the various stressors involved in any given context. In the final analysis, stress is a product of the mind. How I perceive a piece of reality at any moment largely determines my level of stress. In other words, stress does not really cause our tensions and our anxieties. Rather, stress is our reaction to what we perceive out there as demanding something of us. The manner in which we perceive something depends upon a number of variables: our beliefs, our values, our experiences, our upbringing, our education.

This individualized and subjective approach to the basic cause of all stress is difficult to accept; for the most part, we have been taught otherwise, to project stress on our environment, to hold things in our external world as the cause of our tensions or anxieties. For example: "My workload often brings me great stress." "My husband's anger makes me tense." "My wife's forgetfulness makes me anxious." "My boss is always pressuring me."

Before I can have an internal experience of what I have been taught to call stress, I have to evaluate my workload (an intellectual process) and determine such things as time limitations, amount of work to be done, degree of difficulty in doing the work, etc. If my analysis reveals that my workload cannot be successfully and efficiently completed in a reasonable amount of time, then the chances are that I'll say to myself (and to others) that I am unable to do the job in the time allotted, and therefore, I am a failure or incompetent, or something like that. The result will be a growing feeling of stress in the form of blueness perhaps, or frustration, or anger, or any of a number of negative feelings.

The point is that I actually make the decision as to how stressful, if at all, I am going to feel regarding the workload facing me. Perhaps the most significant and simplest way of explaining this lies in these examples: Betty is feeling a great deal of anxiety over her impending physical examination. June also has recently developed similar symptoms and is anticipating a visit to her family physician to have her headaches checked out. She, however, is concerned yet cheerful and optimistic. She feels no dread or anxiety like her friend Betty is suffering.

What makes the difference? Both women are the same age; both have a history of excellent mental and physical health, and so on. Yet one is a wreck, while the other is reasonably worried. One can hardly concentrate on her everyday responsibilities, while the other continues to function effectively.

The difference, obviously, is the way each looks at the situation. This has a great amount to do with the stress level each experiences. In other words, each really manufactures the stress burden they want. Evidently, Betty has decided to be greatly distressed, while June is minimally distressed. It all has to do with you!

Bob and Stan are laid off. Bob flips out and resorts to intensive psychotherapy. Stan spends his free time updating his resume and going to job interviews, convinced he will find employment. Bob is decidedly distressed and pessimistic. Stan is concerned, even worried, but determined to land a job within six months. Each determines his own stress level.

Lucy feels pressured and worn out with secretarial work and raising two youngsters. A single parent with her own parents living on the other side of the country, she has little moral support and is pretty much at her wit's end. Betsy, her fellow-worker in the secretarial pool, is also a single parent with three grade-school children to support. Her parents live relatively close, but are up in years and somewhat dependent on her. She has an older sister and brother who seem to have little time for Betsy and her children.

Betsy feels pressure, and sometimes she wants to run away from it all. But unlike Lucy, Betsy is able to bounce back and keep going; she is positive something will change and she will be able to manage. Lucy gave up her job recently and is looking for something not so stressful. Each determines her own stress level.

What this means is that we have more internal control over stressful reactions than we think. Why else can two people, both in similar situations, react so differently? We manufacture our own stress. Its production is a rational mental activity...and so it can be controlled. Couples enjoying quality marriages somehow know this, not necessarily in the terms I have defined it, but they know it and their behaviors attest to it.

Take Audry and Clint, for example. They are not psychiatrists or psychologists or social scientists of any kind. Audry is a wife, mother of two preschoolers, and a part-time receptionist. Her husband Clint is a self-employed painter and wallpaper hanger, who was having a difficult task making a living at his job. Like so many others in his trade, his income was just not keeping up with the accelerating rate of inflation. It was next to impossible to keep up with the bills, let alone think of buying any extras to make life a little more comfortable.

Audry's widowed grandmother was living with them, a women of eighty-seven years who was fairly well incapacitated and needed a good deal of attention. It seems there was cause for quite a bit of stress in the family. Wrong! Audry and Clint had their moments, true enough, but they controlled their stress reactions to their predicament, rather than the predicament dictating the degree of stress they would experience.

How did they manage? They managed *their way*. First of all, they decided they would not let their predicament get to them, above all else! That may sound rather obvious and simplistic, but not so. There is a certain mind-set that goes along with effective stress management. Many people find themselves quite stressful because they never made a commitment to control their stress levels.

Second, they were deeply spiritual individuals whose belief system included a conviction that prayer is a most powerful ally. They frequently resorted to prayer and meditation and found both a comfort and a relaxing and positive support.

Third, they were able to distinguish (something a good many professional mental health people have difficulty doing) between worry or concern, and rumination. If you asked them what this means, they'd laugh, somewhat embarrassed, and tell you they had no idea what you were talking about. Nevertheless, this elusive psychological feat is exactly what they accomplished.

Dr. Barbara Brown explains it quite clearly in her book, *Supermind*. "Worry or concern is an intellectual act or exercise that begins the problem solving by recognizing the discrepancy between what one expects or hopes for and what one actually perceives."[1] For example, when Clint began his business, he expected (hoped for) to provide his family a reasonably trouble-free income. What he perceived, however, as time went on, was not what he had expected; hence, he had a problem that argued for a solution.

Both he and Audry experienced worry or concern, which motivated them to look for possible solutions to their financial problem. What they were able to avoid, however, is what Dr. Brown refers to as rumination, "that insidious, persistent preoccupation of the mind with pondering, speculating, imagining, and projecting....It is a rehashing and regurgitation of every bit of information about a problem in every conceivable combination, but without success."[2]

Rumination is destructive rather than constructive worry that begins where problem solving is unproductive and frustrated. In less technical jargon, rumination is thinking in circles. We've all had occasion to do this when our intellect has lacked the information needed to solve a problem. Instead of pursuing a rational course toward a solution, it turns into itself, so to speak, and focuses on the stress the problem is causing, allowing negative emotion to flood the mind and halt the reasoning process. This situation can lead to stress-related illness.[3]

Audry and Clint are the first to admit they were not immune to episodes of rumination during those trying times. Yet these episodes were few and far between, yielding little debilitating stress in the long run.

They refused to go around in circles as Clint expressed it. Slowly but surely they took steps to resolve their problem. They sought advice and counsel. They resisted panic when answers were not forthcoming. Both Audry, who is an alcoholic, and Clint hung steadfastly to a prayer she learned during her rehabilitation: "Lord, grant me the courage to change the things I can. The patience to accept those things I cannot change. And the wisdom to know the difference."

# PART TWO

# BASIC BEHAVIORS

## CHAPTER SEVEN

# "Chunking Down" to Quality

We have been educated to deal with the complicated and the intricate so much so that we tend to become easily suspect, sometimes almost paranoid, when confronted with the possibility that the truth frequently arrives in simple dress. Consequently, we all too often tend to shun what is, pan the simplistic, and immerse ourselves in the complex, delighted to be in search of life's mysteries...even where there are none. No wonder our Western mentality finds it so painful to penetrate the Eastern mind.

How unwilling we are to endorse the KISS approach (Keep It Simple, Stupid) to the problem-solving process. The reason has something to do with the adage: "You get what you work for." If it's too easy, you haven't worked for it, so you don't get it. Make it look complicated, intricate, difficult. Then at least you appear to earn your pay. It ties in with the Puritan work ethic and the American way of doing things—the hard way!

Not too long ago Sandy and Paul, two very unhappy people,

came for marriage counseling. Talk about complicating issues; these two were real pros. They were convinced that their relationship was in such dire straits that if marriage counseling were to be effective at all, they would probably be seeing me weekly for the next two years. Not so. It only took a few sessions for them to begin to see the light. And not because of any particular genius of the counsellor. They had simply done what many other couples do; they had magnified their differences and complicated their problems to a point where they were ready to call it quits. They needed someone to lead them through the labyrinth of obstacles to intimacy that they had constructed over seven years of married life.

It actually took the first two sessions before they were willing to consider the *obvious* as the root cause of their relationship problems. What was obvious was that Sandy was a cleaner and Paul was a tidier. When Sandy cleaned the townhouse, the house was cleaned! Every room sparkled. But she put so much into it that she couldn't look at a vacuum cleaner or mop for the next few weeks. Untidiness between cleaning bouts never phased her. Paul, on the other hand, was quite adamant about keeping things in their place at all times. He wasn't into heavy cleaning, but he insisted on tidiness. Books should be on the book shelves, magazines in the rack, shoes in the closet, soiled clothes in the hamper, etc. Dirt behind the refrigerator did not bother him, but used ash trays drove him mad. Pictures should be hung straight, grass cut, weeds pulled, and the bed always made in the morning. Above all, he demanded that the cap be placed back on the toothpaste tube after brushing. Sandy's customary forgetfulness to do so infuriated him, almost as much as did her nightly ritual of washing out her pantyhose and leaving them to dry over the shower curtain rod.

Seven years of attempting to change behavior had failed. She was a slob as far as he was concerned, and she in turn, was fed up with his nit-picking.

Both were doing a tremendous amount of mind reading. He was convinced she was an extremely selfish individual who didn't give a tinker's damn about his needs and evidently had very little, if any, genuine love for him. Sandy, for her part, was certain her husband was twice as neurotic as his mother and should seek psychiatric help. She had no intention of changing her ways and although he never admitted it, she knew all his bitching was his way of getting back at her for working full time. His lack of gratitude and gratefulness for cleaning the house thoroughly once a month appalled her. She felt strongly that she had married a self-centered, egotistical mama's boy who could never be satisfied.

Both had sought legal counsel and were advised to try marriage therapy in a last effort to reconcile their differences.

Their attitudes and behavior toward each other had gotten out of hand by the time I first saw them. Neither one could do anything right as far as the other was concerned. What had started out as a normal difference of opinion about housekeeping methods had gradually degenerated into open warfare. Layer upon layer of mutual blame and grievance built up between them. They were smothering in confusion. Their life together had become so complicated that they had utterly lost sight of what it was that had set them so terribly awry.

Their two youngsters (children have a knack for the obvious!) actually pointed them on the road to recovery. At my request, they accompanied them to the fifth session. I asked the children what they thought was making their parents so unhappy with each other. The older one, Robby, age six, glanced toward them, smiled quickly, then turned full attention to me, his legs swinging nervously and the palms of his hands spread flat against the seat on each side of his erect body. He replied with surprising force, "Mommy and Daddy love each other. But they'd be happier if they did what they tell us to do."

"And what is that?" I inquired, almost in a whisper. I was afraid to speak any louder for fear of scaring him.

Andy, the five year old, turned to speak, jumping in over his brother and tearfully crying out, "They shouldn't call each other names! They tell us not to!"

Then it was Robby's turn. "And they shouldn't pick on each other. They get mad when Andy and I pick on each other."

I gently prodded them. "What do you guys think your mommy and daddy should do?"

Andy was the quicker. "I just told you. They should like each other and be happy."

I turned to Robby. "How about you? What do you think?" Robby stood up, walked over to his dad, hugged him, then sidled over to his mother, squirmed up on her lap, looked at me and said, "I think Mommy should put her shoes in the closet, and when she forgets, Daddy should do it for her."

"How many times should Daddy do it?" I asked.

"All the time," he replied, looking sideways at his father, a tiny bit apprehensive.

"You mean every time your mommy forgets, your daddy should put her shoes away?" I asked.

"Yeh," he answered. "Just like Daddy wants me to always help Andy when he forgets to zipper his pants."

"What else?" I urged them.

Robby was on a roll. "Mommy should come home on time from work and help Daddy straighten up. Daddy works hard too, you know."

That was the beginning of progress for the couple. Their children helped them get back to the basics. Although it wasn't easy, Paul and Sandy gradually untangled their complicated relationship, reconciled themselves to what was, and learned to practice some of what they so easily preached to their boys. "Out of the mouths of babes...."

Sandy and Paul discovered, or rather re-discovered, that there is no mystery to a satisfying and lasting conjugal relationship...but there is work, mixed with a bit of magic here and there.

Perhaps the single, most important piece of learning they gleaned from their counseling sessions was how couples growing quality relationships KISS—they chunk down and they chunk up! That is, they break a problem down into its components and then, having examined them and dealt with them, put the pieces back together.

George and Dottie are an excellent example of a chunking couple who KISS their problems away. They learned to chunk early in their marriage. They are the first to admit, however, that in the beginning of their relationship, chunking was quite foreign to their problem-solving strategies. They had a tendency to do what most poor problem solvers do. In their haste to resolve the difficulty (whatever it may be) poor problem solvers usually attempt to handle the entire conflict all at once. In so doing, they try to force a solution on the problem, hoping it will heal all wounds. More often than not, it only intensifies the painful situation.

Chunking down, on the other hand, is done by effective problem solvers who face a problem of some magnitude. They look at the "big picture" and realize they have to break it down into smaller or more manageable chunks.

That is what George and Dottie learned to do. They speak of a situation in their relationship some years ago when they KISSed it away by chunking down and then chunking up.

It seems that George and Dottie were at their wits' end about what to do with their deteriorating retail business and their twin teenage daughters who were fast becoming severe discipline problems both at home and at school. On top of that, they were feeling guilty about the time and effort they were putting into the business to the neglect, as they saw it, of their children. They were obviously overwhelmed by it all and unfortunately, it was beginning to severely affect their relationship. They could not come to terms on what to do, spending much of their time disagreeing on most everything. The ripple effect was setting in, and they were finding fault with each other constantly.

At that point, they began to chunk it. "It was either chunk or be sunk!" First they decided what chunk merited top priority. That decision was practically a given. They had become sparring partners. Something had to be done about that, and right away; otherwise, there was no way the other parts of the problem could be resolved to everyone's satisfaction. So they tackled their relationship problem initially, well aware, of course, that the other parts had to be tended to also, but not with the concentrated effort they put into "the getting to be pals once again," as Dottie nicely recalls.

The "how to" followed naturally. They discussed various ways to restore this "palship," decided upon several deliberate moves, and proceeded to work at them. One of the moves was to spend more time listening to each other and leveling honestly. That meant George had to resist the temptation to spend large amounts of time at the business, and Dottie had to be willing to take time from her desperate parenting efforts to communicate more effectively with her husband. This combined effort to remediate and enhance their conjugal relationship was not easy. The temptation to try to resolve the children's situation and their retail problems as well was almost too much to resist at first.

For example, on one occasion they had made arrangements to spend a weekend by themselves, something they had rarely done in recent years. The children objected because they wanted their parents to take them to the shore. Ordinarily, George and Dottie would have met their daughters' request, hoping that they would appreciate their parents' generosity and that, in turn, would be reflected in their improved behavior. This time, however, the parents stood their ground, as difficult as it was, and left the youngsters with Dottie's sister. Afterwards they reported that, with the exception of the first few worrisome hours of the trip, they enjoyed themselves very much. Each felt a growing pride in the other for standing their ground. Each started to feel that old familiar sense of us-ness once again, and the mutual respect and trust they had known earlier began to resurface.

And a funny thing happened on the way to their relationship enhancement! Ever so slowly, but definitely, the children quieted down, became more relaxed, and began to display a much greater sense of responsibility and cooperation at home and in school. The correlation is clear. It's called modeling! As the parents went, so went the children.

Such correlations are common when a couple chunks down effectively. This makes sense when you realize that the parts of a problem are usually related and that by focusing successfully on any one part, you influence the others.

George and Dottie also experienced this with regard to the deteriorating retail business. Once he was feeling better about himself, Dottie, and the children, he was able to arrive at a decision about the business. It was a decision, he had known for a long time, that was the only sensible way to go, but he had hesitated to take the necessary steps because he already felt he had failed at being a husband and father. To give up the business and start again was too much to face. But with a renewed self-esteem and much encouragement and support from the family, he finally let go, much to the relief of all concerned.

After that it was simply a matter of chunking up again, i.e., putting all the pieces back together. In this case it was done in one evening, more or less, when they sat around the kitchen table and reviewed what had happened to them during the past year and how each of them contributed to the resolution of their family problems and the enhancement of their family relations.

CHAPTER EIGHT

# Empowering Each Other

Habit formation is the enemy of valuing, and valuing your partner is essential to a quality relationship.[1] When couples first fall in love, valuing each other and openly expressing one's appreciation of the other's behavior is relatively easy and frequently forthcoming. As time goes on, however, one of the hazards of getting used to each other is habit formation with the consequent reduction or even loss of awareness of your spouse's previously valued behavior.

Once this awareness is lost, expressions of appreciation and admiration are replaced with silence. And even if you still notice them, chances are your responses are far less enthusiastic and genuine than before, because you have come to take things for granted.

Habit formation is a natural, necessary, and very human phenomenon. Just imagine what it would be like if we were unable to form habits and perform a multitude of behaviors at a more or less unconscious or spontaneous level of awareness. Driving a car is a perfect example. Suppose, instead of applying the brakes, accelerating, steering, etc., automatically in a usual traffic pattern (habit formation through conditioning), we had to stop and think about every detail and every move we made as we did when we were first learning to drive. Each time we got behind the wheel we would have to learn all over again! I wonder how many of us would be driving as regularly as we do. Habit formation is a time saver and an energy conserver, to say the least.

Yet like most things in our world, it is good news and not so good news. The not so good news is that we can become accustomed to something that is repetitious, take it for granted, and that something can lose its significance and value quite inadvertently.

Kate for many years has cooked liver in the same succulent, delicious, tender way she has from the beginning of our marriage. This is no easy feat, as those of you who like liver will readily agree. About six months ago I noticed that liver was escaping the menu more and more. When I inquired about its absence, she informed me that recently she thought I was tired of eating it. I asked her somewhat sarcastically how she came by this disturbing piece of mind reading. Equally sarcastically she retorted that for the last year or so I said very little if anything positive about her liver dinners, so she interpreted my silence as growing disapproval or disinterest!

Interesting, isn't it? Through habit formation I came to expect a liver meal par excellence, and eventually took it for granted. Kate, on the other hand, did a similar trick. She came to expect a demonstration of appreciation (valuing), and when it was not forthcoming, she noticed its absence! As she added up those times with no feedback, she eventually concluded I no longer liked her liver specialty particularly. Hence, she stopped cooking it.

A small misunderstanding? Perhaps. But my expression of appreciation had come to mean much to her. As she explained, it motivated her to do her best in other ways as well, besides cooking. She felt confident and good about herself and our relationship. In effect, she felt empowered by her husband's honest admiration of her culinary skills, and it had a ripple effect on other things she did. She grew accustomed to its energizing effect, and when I stopped stroking her in this fashion, she began to add up the times I no longer responded and innocently, although incorrectly, concluded I was tired of the liver menu.

Until I approached her on the matter, she was working in the dark as to the reasons for my silence. Without feedback from me (who was still unaware), she did not have enough information to make a valid and reliable conclusion. (Mind reading was the result.) Was I just tired of liver but hesitant to tell her? Was she actually losing her touch, and did it show with other meals she cooked and other things, but I wasn't saying anything? How come, in recent months, I seemed to be so anxious to eat out? And so on.

Our happy resolution of the misunderstanding prevented what might have eventually become a more pervasive misunderstanding, for Kate was beginning to form a belief about me that was, until then, foreign to her way of evaluating my intentions and actions. She admitted she was starting to think I might be losing interest in her! This conjecture arose not only from the number of times she noticed I had no particular comment to make about her cooking, but also from the number of times she added up other things that were no longer happening, like complimenting her on her make-up, her dressing up, her social graces, her money-saving shopping tours.

One may be tempted to conclude that Kate is too emotionally dependent upon continual confirmation of her behavior. Not by a long shot! She is healthily independent; just human, that's all. And like most of us normal humans who want to be empowered from time to time by our spouses, she too looks for the nod of approval, the smile, the touch, the words of appreciation and admiration. As I do!

Her only mistake was mind reading for so long a time. Had she brought her concern to my attention sooner, she could have saved herself a good bit of discomfort. But Kate is marvelously human like the rest of us, and on occasion mind reading is a favorite indoor sport for most of us.

The authors of the best selling book, *One Minute Manager*, stress that an effective leader praises a staff member's valued behavior.[2] This "people management principle" is obviously grounded in human experience. Who does not react positively to genuine praise! Who does not feel empowered when we are honestly recognized for our accomplishments! Who is not willing to go the extra mile when we know our efforts are valued and appreciated!

The opposite reaction is also obvious when praise is continually withheld and our efforts meet with little or no approval. Gradual apathy, indifference, resentment, and even hostility can and usually does build inside us, only to eventually be released in some negative fashion.

I once worked for a small company whose people management strategy was basically this: As long as you are doing your job productively, you will never hear from the managers. If you are not doing your job productively, you will hear from them immediately! Employee morale was extremely poor, except among a few favorites of the company president. The managers were true to their word; they left us alone as long as we produced. Never once did my manager meet with me to express how good he felt about some specific achievement of mine in behalf of the company. I do recall, however, the times he reprimanded my inefficiencies and highlighted my failures, even as he frequently did with other staff members.

To this day, and that was many years ago, whenever I think about it, I still feel a tinge of the resentment and smothering humiliation that was gradually eating away at me while I worked for this company. I finally had to leave because a couple of frightening things were happening to me. One was the growing sense of self-depreciation I was experiencing as I stacked into my memory occasion after occasion when my successes were met with silence and my mistakes were met with bombastic reprisals.

The other thing I feared was the covert behavior I began to indulge in in retaliation. I began to sabotage the operation, and I was not alone! Unexpected illness, lateness, increasing mistakes, forgetfulness, missed deadlines, etc., were a few of the ways we gained our revenge. A couple of years after my departure, the company closed...productivity had come to a virtual standstill, and high employee turnover finally led to impossible operating costs.

Most couples who have poor quality relationships have a similar attitude toward empowering one another as my manager had toward his staff. Almost without exception, the people who come to me for counseling have somehow lost sight of the need to empower each other through honest valuing and praising. They rarely hear from each other unless it has to do with negative performance evaluation. In marriage, we commonly call such evaluation fault-finding (and rightly so).

I sometimes request husbands and wives in counseling to take a sheet of paper, draw a vertical line down the center, and list as many power points of their partner on the left side as they can think of, and then as many limitations as they can think of on the right side. Power points are attitudes and behaviors a partner possesses that the other feels are worthy of recognition and appreciation. Limitations are simply attitudes and behaviors that, while not necessarily wrong, bad, or unacceptable to others in different contexts, are unacceptable to one's spouse in the context of their relationship and therefore call for reprimand of some sort or other.

Often enough this simple exercise becomes quite an eye opener, especially when one or the other or both find they have little to record in the way of power points. Of course, the principal intent of the exercise is to get them thinking about this whole matter of empowering each other, a strategy for relating that can effectively reduce and hopefully blow away the apathy and indifference that has crept into the marriage.

It does happen, however, that this exercise on occasion reveals that the limitations far surpass in number and intensity the power points of one or both individuals. I always feel sad when this evaluation materializes, because it usually indicates that the disintegration of the relationship has gone past reconstruction, and the end may be just around the corner.

In effect, it is no longer a matter of just taking the other for granted, or negative habit formation that we all fall into from time to time. Unfortunately, it now reveals a drastic change in perspective on the part of one or both to the extent that they are convinced their differences are irreconcilable because their limitations so overwhelm their power points. They are painfully aware of this and have no hope for change in the future. They have long passed the point of mutual flexibility wherein each can and will accommodate their needs and expectations to those of the other. Sad, indeed, whenever it occurs!

Empowering each other is something couples enjoying quality marriages do very well. They take each other for granted at times, and they fall prey to negative habit formation occasionally, but because they are capable of giving each other constructive feedback, they become aware of these deficiencies more readily and take steps to correct them as soon as possible. It's called working at one's marriage.

The "How to Praise People" model that the *One Minute Manager* proposes in relation to the work environment, with a little adjustment, can be aptly applied to the conjugal setting as well. The authors offer a seven-step method:[3]

1. Tell people up front that you are going to let them know how they are doing.
2. Praise people immediately.
3. Tell people what they did right. Be specific.
4. Tell people how good you feel about what they did right and how it helps the organization and the other people who work there.
5. Stop for a moment of silence to let them feel how good you feel.
6. Encourage them to do more of the same.
7. Shake hands or touch people in a way that makes it clear that you support their success in the organization.

This method is one of the secrets that an effective manager uses in motivating his or her staff. Is it a case of covert manipulation? The answer depends upon the circumstances and intention of the praiser. If you offer unfounded praise with the hope that you can get someone on the ball, that is manipulation, covert or otherwise. If, however, you praise valued behavior that is observable, and you truly appreciate it and hope it will continue, this is what the *One Minute Manager* is proposing: honest approval and genuine motivation.

Whether or not they are aware of the sequence of steps they follow in empowering each other, husbands and wives who grow satisfying and lasting relationships do follow, with some variation, the method outlined.

*1. From the start they let each other know what they appreciate and value about the other's behavior.*

Tina and Rick began their mutual admiration society, as their friends jokingly put it, shortly after they met. Tina was impressed with Rick's communication skills and told him she especially enjoyed being with him at social gatherings. He, in turn, let Tina know from the beginning he was delighted with her athletic ability and was particularly proud of her tennis game.

As other valued traits appeared in each one, both were only too ready to openly express their admiration to the point where it became second nature to them. They are married twenty-two years now, and their friends still remark about their mutual admiration society.

Tina and Rick are a far cry from those couples who deliberately hold back approval from each other. I think one of the most asinine things I've ever heard is the remark "I like the way she dresses, but I'll never tell her or she'll get a big head!" That's about as Archie Bunker as you can get. And it's just as stupid as my former manager's slogan: "Don't praise or they'll ask for a raise!"

*2. Couples in quality marriages praise each other immediately, or as soon as possible.*

Dr. Thomas Connellan, in his book *How to Grow People into Self-Starters*, stresses the importance of this step in empowering others through legitimate praise. He states that reinforce-

ment (praise) should be as immediate as possible to be most effective and most powerful. Praise that is withheld for any
length of time doesn't do much in the way of encouraging (empowering) a person to continue a valued behavior.[4]

He readily admits, however, that immediacy is not always
an option, but whenever possible it should be used. Praise can,
no doubt, be used immediately more often than not in the marital relationship.

How often counselors hear this kind of dialogue in our offices:

Husband:    No question about it. She's fantastic when it
            comes to taking care of our everyday finances.

Wife:       I can't believe you said that.

Husband:    What do you mean? You know that's what I've
            always felt.

Wife:       That's the first time in years you've admitted
            it. Most of the time you're on me for the mis-
            takes I make.

Husband:    That's nonsense. What did I just tell you the
            other day when...

Wife:       You mean how glad you were that I kept up
            with our family Christmas club? Hell, George,
            Christmas was eight months ago. Why didn't
            you tell me then?

Husband:    Oh, well, I thought you knew how I felt.

Put quite simply, if and when you genuinely praise someone,
you are not only expressing your appreciation or approval, you
are also encouraging the person to keep up the good work. This
is the motivational aspect of praise, which empowers a person
to continue to repeat or sustain his or her valued behavior. Only
if the praise follows the act within a reasonable time span does
it have its desired effect.

3. *Telling your partner what he or she did right in specific terms
is not always necessary in the intimacy of a marital relationship,
but it is always the "more certain" way to go.*

By "more certain" I mean there is less risk of misunderstanding and greater chance of empowering the husband or wife ef-

fectively. How so? To explain, I need to first define what I mean by specific terms. Let's take Andy and Ronnie as a study.

Andy is married to Betty. He frequently applauds her in private and public. He says things like "Wow, you're the best!" Or, "Honey, they don't come any sharper than you!" Or, "Sweetheart, you're my angel. You do everything just the way I like it!"

Is there something wrong with what Andy is trying to convey to Betty? Would that many spouses would at least say that much in praise of the other! However, what is Andy saying to Betty? She likes what Andy says, but there's that little irritating voice inside her that keeps whispering, "Hey, what is he talking about? What does he want next?"

Ronnie's way of honestly praising her husband, Seth, is different. She expresses it exactly as she sees it. "Seth, as long as we've been married, I never cease to be amazed at the patience you have driving in all that traffic when we are coming back from the shore on Sunday nights. You don't lean on the horn; you don't push to get ahead. You simply sit back, relax, and make me feel like I don't have to get uptight. I can enjoy the ride."

There is no way Seth can miss that message. There is little risk of misunderstanding (unless Seth is suffering from paranoia!); and chances are he will continue his calm driving, which Ronnie apparently loves, because she has nicely anchored it in his memory bank. She has empowered him in regard to this specific behavior.

4. *The* One Minute Manager *recommends that managers tell people how they feel about what they did right and how it affects others. This step is most appropriate for couples striving to grow quality relationships.*

Unfortunately, our well-meaning Andy overlooked this step in the how-to-praise-people model. He really did not tell Betty how he felt about what she was doing that pleased him. Reread what Andy said and you'll agree. "Honey, they don't come any sharper than you!" says nothing to Betty about Andy's internal state...what exactly he was feeling.

It is in the open expression of one's feelings that makes the difference and gets the message across. Had Andy said that he really felt secure with this particular financial investment because Betty was so sharp in this specific area, it would have made a world of difference to her. Had he added that her reasonable risk-taking skills were rubbing off on their two teenage youngsters, she would have also gotten the added message that her behavior was helping the whole family.

5. *Then stop for a moment of silence to let them feel how you feel.*

This takes a bit of stage presence, knowing when to pause and allow your message to sink in. I know a good many husbands and wives who are good "pausers" in this regard.

I met with a couple who needed counseling in relation to one of their teenage daughters. The wife was extremely guilt-ridden over the child's drug addiction and found it most difficult to contain herself. As I listened, the husband tried to reassure her by praising her for her continual efforts to raise their three youngsters successfully, citing example after example of her persistence in doing what was best for them. Then he paused, after telling her how much he loved and respected her for her efforts.

The pause was equally effective as the words. There was at least two minutes of complete silence. Then she broke into a smile, reached for his hand, and slowly shook her head in acknowledgment and gratitude for his encouragement.

6. *This step has to do with encouragement, which is the essence of empowering your spouse. You encourage your loved one to do more of the same.*

As much as she wanted to, Jill was scared to death at the thought of going back to college. Dan encouraged her time and again to do so. At his insistence, she finally consented to take a couple of night courses "just to try it" to see how she would do. She did exceptionally well with one course and struggled to a passing grade with the other. Being the person she was, she focused on her poorer performance rather than on the excellent one.

Dan praised her for the work she put into both courses and encouraged her to continue. She decided to risk it. He was a proud husband the day she graduated. That happened thirty-five years ago. To this day, Jill lovingly speaks of how her husband made her the professional business woman she turned out to be.

*7. This final step in the* One Minute Manager's *model has to do with physical touch, shaking hands, or touching in some supportive fashion.*

People in quality relationships are touchers to begin with. They reach out often to each other, in private or in public, so it is natural for them to make physical contact, especially when they are empowering each other. A hug, a kiss, an arm around the waist, a hand on the shoulder, a pinch on the posterior, any of a hundred ways to reinforce one's words with a gesture. So often the physical contact is more potent than even the words.

I was on one occasion in conference with a couple on the verge of splitting up. They had been living together for five years, and now he was pushing to get married. But she was quite hesitant. Their frequent arguments over the matter had brought them to the point of "either we get married or we split for good."

Why her hesitancy? Several reasons, actually. But the one that kept popping up in the discussion was the fact that he rarely touched her outside the bedroom. She felt she was a woman who thrived on physical demonstrations of affection besides just sex! A few direct questions to him revealed that such was pretty much the case. He loved her, enjoyed sex with her, wanted to marry her, but was not the touchy, feely type of person, as he described it. He complained that she was always looking for a hug, a kiss, a touch of some kind every time he turned around.

I had known the woman on a personal basis for a number of years and always found her to be a mature, level-headed, intelligent person who was very kinesthetic, a healthy feeling person, to say the least. As we continued to talk, another variable in their relationship surfaced; she complained that he never (rarely) praised her for her accomplishments. In defending himself against this accusation, he admitted to me that he wasn't brought up to praise others, especially for what they are expected to do! And besides, "she should know by now how I feel about her!"

At the conclusion of the session, I strongly suggested they either work with me (or some other counselor) on improving their accommodation skills and hope for improvement, or split up for good. Arguing about who was right and who was wrong was getting them nowhere. It never gets anyone anywhere.

This lack of empowering one's partner through words and actions is standard fare at the table of troubled relationships. Invariably, either husband or wife or both are unaware or refuse to praise and encourage the other. And many times it is a case of the chicken or the egg. Is this couple in the throes of marital distress because they did not empower, or did their unwillingness to acknowledge each other's accomplishment come after they found themselves in distress? Either way, the problem is real and must be dealt with. It is a problem that discourages people from accommodating—*the key to quality marriage.*

## CHAPTER NINE

# The Need to Flip-Flop

There is no question about it. If you want a quality marriage, then get ready to *flip-flop* regularly. If you can't or won't, you'll probably have to settle for less...or nothing.

Freddy and Helen are excellent flip-floppers. He did not want Helen to work full time until the children were older. He reminded her more than once that he came from a family who adamantly believed a mother's place is at the side of the little ones through young adolescence. Then, *maybe,* a mother can work *part time!*

Helen, of course, thought otherwise, and offered her husband a proposal that substantiated her need to reenter the world of work, and reasonably guaranteed the security of the children.

Freddy listened to her, considered what she had to say, understood her position, questioned her on certain unclear points, reiterated his own position, explained to her that he was certain it would not work out the way she anticipated, told her she really ought to back off for a while...then flip-flopped.

Freddy and I had a drink together a couple nights later. He told me the story. When I gently inquired about his flip-flop, he broke into laughter, the deep belly-laugh kind. It was one of those contagious healthy laughs, when you know he is laughing at himself and really enjoying it, and you jump right in, and at the end you're both exhausted!

When he stopped laughing he explained. "With all my huffin' and puffin' about the kids' safety and my values, and her lack of updated skills in the marketplace, I suddenly realized she wanted to do it! Wow, did that hit me right between the eyes! Regardless of all my objections, she wanted to do it, and she would do her best to make it work. What I'm really laughing about," he went on to explain, "is the utter stupidity of my position. And if I didn't laugh, I'd probably choke!"

"Choke on what?" I asked.

"On the fact that, with all due respect to kids and how I was brought up and all the other stuff, where I'm really at is our relationship. The relationship is bottom line. And I'm laughing at my stupidity because six years ago I wanted to go into business for myself, and she said I should go for it. So I did, in spite of the fact that our financial situation was anything but secure, and her health was poor at the time. And that stuff about coming from a family that believed mom's place is in the home? Well, they also believed that you don't risk just about everything to go into business for yourself. Funny, isn't it! When the shoe was on the other foot, what they thought didn't matter to me! The hypocrisy of my position, that's a better word than stupidity, hit me right between the eyes as we were arguing. That's when I suddenly and willingly flip-flopped."

Freddy went on to recall that, at first, Helen had shown strong resistance to his wanting to go into business for himself. Her father had tried it and went bankrupt. But she placed herself in Freddy's shoes, and despite some lingering fears, flip-flopped and told him to go for it.

Helen's flip-flop came about because she was able to see the proposed business venture from her husband's frame of reference, and because she knew her consent could only enhance their relationship.

Helen and Freddy are effective flip-floppers for at least two reasons: They are able to evaluate issues from each other's perspective, and they value the continual enhancement of their relationship as bottom line. Nothing is more important than the growth of their marriage. Therefore, they and other couples like them can accommodate to each other more easily. Flip-flopping is the skill required to accommodate, and accommodation is the *key* to a quality relationship. Without it, you may have a marriage by force of circumstances, but you don't have a mutually satisfying, nor chances are, a lasting one.

And just what is it to accommodate? One definition is "to make room for." I like that one; it is a most appropriate metaphor for what accommodation means in marriage. Helen and Freddy make room for each other's needs by flip-flopping in each other's interest and in the interest of the relationship.

"Making room for" each other's needs, wants, values, and beliefs goes beyond mere compromise or trade-off. And it certainly goes far beyond competition, which is the very antithesis of accommodation.

To compromise or trade off in a marital setting is not necessarily a bad thing. In many circumstances, it is the only way a couple can get unstuck and resolve whatever is causing their conflict. However, compromising and trading off rightfully belong in the marketplace. Too much of these in marriage turns the conjugal relationship into a business.

Many couples who seek counseling are having trouble flip-flopping because they consider it totally a matter of compromising or trading-off. With this attitude, a couple of conflictual situations usually arise.

1. *Keeping Score.* One spouse or the other begins to "keep score" and the game playing commences. "You didn't go along with me when I wanted to, so I don't agree to what you want now."

Sheri was a scorekeeper. She came into counseling when she added up the score and found that she had flip-flopped much more than Brad. Naturally, she felt like a loser. My reaction to her report was agreement. She had evolved into a "forever-giver-inner." The idea of compromise had become quite abhorrent to her.

Brad, on the other hand, had not kept score, so her eventual confrontation came as a big surprise to him. He was under the impression that they were dancing very nicely together! Compromising or trading-off can lead to this sort of confusion...and worse.

2. *Piece of Turf.* The "piece of turf" game frequently occurs. It begins quite innocently and properly. Early in the marriage Diane and Philip decided to divide responsibilities. Consequently they structured their flip-flopping rather closely. They divided the decision-making process: Philip handled the finances, which meant that Diane flip-flopped to his value judgments in this specific area, while she made the decisions related to child rearing with him flip-flopping to her way of thinking. And so on.

With few exceptions, this approach inevitably runs into trouble. Why? Ideas, beliefs, values gradually change, and this phenomenon invites the invasion of each other's turf.

"Hey, Philip, I think we should invest in x and sell."

"Listen, Diane, I think the children should do their homework before dinner. And don't forget who handles the money around here."

"OK, just you remember whose job it is to see to the kids' homework, so butt out!"

And so on.

This piece of turf game is the stuff of which business management is made, departmentalization. It is an especially popular game between the engineering department and the marketing department in many manufacturing companies.

Generally speaking, this structure or arrangement works rather well, in spite of the inter-departmental conflicts that arise over whose responsibility is whose. In large measure that is because there is usually an in-house arbitrator whose job it is to reconcile departmental differences and assign responsibility when and where necessary.

In marriage, however, this piece of turf game can be debilitating. What started out as a conjugal partnership soon disintegrates into a sparring partnership. This is flip-flopping at its worst!

Accommodation through mutual flip-flopping also goes far beyond *competition*. If there is one variable that is insidious to the marriage us-ness, it is the matter of competing values between spouses. As a matter of fact, the primary cause of marital discord and strife is values collisions or competition. It is the very antithesis of accommodation. When a couple competes, they become, as Webster's explains, "rivals in a contest." And when you are a contestant, it is next to impossible to make room for your rival's needs, wants, values, and beliefs.

Competition in the marketplace is the heart of the matter in a free enterprise system. Obviously it is the *sine qua non* in the field of sports. And a light-hearted competitive approach to personal achievement between husband and wife is certainly appropriate on occasion. But the win-lose style of competition that pervades many marital relationships is the issue I am presently addressing. This kind of spousal competition, which is the primary cause of marital discord, results from the inability of partners to flip-flop their way to mutual accommodation.

Competition, for better or for worse, is a way of life for all of us. We learn to compete from day one, but it is not always good news. Competition motivates people, gives them direction and a sense of self-esteem and well-being, helps them set goals and acquire the necessary discipline to achieve these goals, provides the opportunity for them to actualize their potential, earns them the right to influence and lead those who wish to model them...and a thousand other benefits.

In our society we reward those who compete. Those who win get more rewards; but even those who lose are usually appropriately compensated. Our heroes evolve through and in competition, and rightly so. They are willing to risk, to put their futures on the line. Whether in fantasy or reality, we love to emulate their courage and model our behavior after theirs, no matter what field of endeavor they are associated with.

Even (and long before professional football) religions taught us the need to compete and the concurrent need to model our lives after the heroes of godliness. Angels and Satan, good and evil, heaven and hell, saints and sinners, angels and demons were a few of the competitive dichotomies presented to us for consideration.

So it would seem that competition is very much a part of the human condition. No small wonder, then, that the love that originally drew two people together in us-ness is so often and so soon overshadowed by a competitiveness that so often and so soon threatens the quality of their relationship.

What is not so good about competitiveness within marriage? No matter how good a sport one may be, no one really likes to lose! We have a hundred ways of consoling a loser: "Better luck next time." "Keep your chin up, your turn will come." "Remember, it's only a game." "It takes a big person to admit defeat." The fact remains, however, that the one who loses is a loser at that particular time. There may be resigned losers, and courageous losers, and forward-looking losers, and nice-guy losers; but I've never met a happy and contented loser. Losing means you goofed, made a mistake, failed, someone bettered you, made you less than, and so forth. When you lose (depending, of course, on the seriousness of the loss and the frequency of losing) you may feel impotent, insignificant, useless, like nothing, ignorant, stupid, foolish, or any of countless negative, self-defeating ways.

One professional athlete whose team lost a championship was reported as saying that the experience of coming so close to victory only to meet with defeat made him realize that winning wasn't the ultimate reward in a contest. Rather, it was the ability to accept failure and still hold one's head high. What the reporters did not know was that for approximately a week after the news interview, this man was continually intoxicated to the point where his manager assigned him a bodyguard to protect him against himself! He was so horribly depressed over the loss, he couldn't face life. What we say about losing, and what we feel and do are frequently two different things. All of which is to repeat: No one really likes to lose!

Most of us can tolerate occasional losses. We do have a threshold or tolerance maximum, however. Once we go over that threshold, all kinds of psychological repercussions can occur.

Many of the people who come for marriage counseling have gone over the threshold in conjugal competition. They see themselves as perpetual losers and their spouses as perennial winners. They are beaten down, discouraged, despondent, resentful, and feel impotent to do anything about it. In most cases, one of my therapeutic strategies is to attempt to establish or reestablish parity between the partners. Not infrequently, both husband and wife feel like losers in relation to each other.

Janet and Drew are a case in point. Married only two years, each felt that the other was anything but accommodating. Neither saw the other as a genuine flip-flopper; both were over the threshold. Each was able to present me with a win-lose list of incidents which, in their minds, supported their contention that life with the other was a long series of losses (therefore, victories for the other).

The first interview revealed that this situation had only gradually developed within the last six to eight months and had only recently taken on catastrophic proportions. The idea that they had unwittingly established a pattern of competitiveness between them never occurred to them. They came to counseling blaming each other for their recurring conflicts over who is right by reason of his or her stubbornness, bullheadedness, selfishness, inconsiderateness. They had a values collision, and you could cut their competitiveness with a knife.

Take, for example, the issue of housing. Janet insisted they buy a house rather than remain living any longer with Drew's parents. She was four months pregnant with their first child and dearly wanted to have her own home. Besides, she argued, it was time they begin to build equity for their future. But Drew was equally adamant about remaining where they were until he solidified his sales position with the company he had recently joined. Besides, as he in turn argued, they could save that much more money toward a down payment and reduce the monthly mortgage payments. Janet accused Drew of free-loading on his parents, and he accused her of placing material things before their love for each other.

Janet considered Drew to be a Simon Legree when it came to saving, while he viewed his wife as being addicted to spending. Drew did tend to be more conservative, not only regarding money, but in most matters related to their lives. Janet was a risk taker and tended to live for the day. Their marriage had become a battleground, each trying to win over the other to his or her way of thinking. They had reached a point when just about everything became an issue. Each was drained from the escalating conflicts; each felt more and more like a loser. Neither was willing to accommodate. They were in the throes of marital competition. Flip-flopping was the last thing they had in mind. They were indeed over the threshold and were convinced their differences could never be resolved. They viewed their plight as the sad result of a terrible mismatch and considered their discrepancies in values and beliefs irreconcilable.

Janet and Drew did not persist in counseling. They separated and eventually divorced, convinced that the other one was too bull-headed and stubborn to admit he or she was wrong. What they, and so many other couples like them, were unaware of was the fact that they had unwittingly set up a pattern of competition early in their relationship; and because accommodation through flip-flopping was out of the question in their minds (because each firmly believed he or she was right!), they judged their differences irreconcilable rather than see that their differences were largely based upon misinformation and misunderstanding about their individual needs and wants.

Even quality marriages have discrepancies in individual wants and needs, which cause conflicts and discord from time to time. After all, even quality marriages are composed of people who like to win, hate to lose, and don't mind a bit of competitiveness on occasion!

However, the essential difference between the Janets and Drews of the world and the quality relationship that Spenser and Hildy enjoy lies in the fact that this latter couple recog-

nize that when they are neck and neck over an issue with neither one wanting to budge an inch, *the relationship must break
the tie; the us-ness in their marriage takes priority.* The result is
that they rarely compete for a solution to their conflict. Rather
they flip-flop, accommodate, and cooperate in the problem-
solving process.

Couples like Spenser and Hildy understand that there are
very few instances where one partner is all right and the other all
wrong. Ordinarily, it's a matter of how one sees and feels about
an issue. As a professor of mine once said, "The reason people
have values collisions is simply because everyone has his own
idea of a good time." Most marital conflicts arise from value differences, not actual rights or wrongs. And a value is really nothing more than the importance one places upon something at any
given moment.

Spenser likes to tell the story of the time when he and Hildy were
at loggerheads over a decision as to where to spend their long-
awaited vacation away from the children for the first time. He insisted they go someplace where they would not have to move
around or travel much, yet be able to enjoy the things they liked to
do together. Hildy was convinced they were in need of doing something entirely different for a change. After all, she argued, they
could play golf right at home. She voted for an automobile trip
across country to visit his parents in San Francisco. It would be her
first time to really see the USA.

Each, according to Spenser, pleaded his or her case, sighting
all the right things about his or her proposal, as well as what
was "all wrong" with the other's reasoning. Suddenly Hildy
smiled, then broke into laughter, and barely managed to ex-
claim quite excitedly, "Spense, I've thought over what you are
saying and what I am saying, and my irrefutable conclusion is
that we are both right, and we are both wrong! Now what do
we do?"

As Spenser tells it, at that instant he felt he loved his wife
more than in all their twenty years of marriage. He, too, began to
laugh and immediately they were off their chairs and into each
other's arms.

As they embraced, Hildy quietly suggested they ditch both their plans and start over again. Spenser agreed, and an hour later they were phoning the local travel agent to make arrangements for a Carribean cruise. Spenser loved that idea because he had an option about moving around. Once he was on board he could stay on board or go sightseeing at the various ports-of-call. Hildy would not see the good old USA, but she would fulfill an equally personal need to sight-see and "expand her horizons," as she said. As for golf and tennis, Spenser agreed, "You can do that at home anytime."

I like Spenser's final observation. "If you want a successful marriage, remember, *breaking even is winning!*"

## CHAPTER TEN

# Put Your Ears on a Stick

"Synergy" means working together. In the field of medicine, it has always been used to describe the working together of two or more drugs in such a way that the result is a new drug or medication that is greater in effect than the sum of the drugs taken independently. "The whole is greater than the sum of its parts."

As applied to marriage, the word is used to describe the working together of husband and wife in such a way that the result is a cooperative and harmonious environment which, in turn, not only produces a mutually satisfying and lasting relationship, but promotes a sense of personal well-being, achievement, and self-realization.

Some time ago I came across a quotation that aptly describes this concept of synergy: "Snowflakes are one of nature's most fragile things, but just look at what they can do when they stick together...."[1]

Sticking together means communicating effectively. This

chapter deals with the listening part of effective communication. The title of the chapter comes from my childhood. Whenever my grandmother wanted us youngsters to really listen to her, she would preface her message with these words: "All right, children, I have something to tell you, so put your ears on a stick and listen real hard!" And more often than not, we did just that. Not only did she capture our attention with her opening directive, but we knew when she finished that one of us would be called upon to play it back to her. Woe to the one who could not do it!

To this day I am deeply grateful for being taught how to listen instead of merely being told to listen. Our schools have long taught us the three "R's." Somehow or other, I believe most of us were shortchanged. No one seemed to think of teaching us how to listen, yet so much of our information comes to us by way of the spoken word.

I am also indebted to Thomas Gordon, Ph.D., founder and president of Effectiveness Training, Inc., who through his publications and seminars "spread the gospel" of effective communication.[2]

Many of the personal problems that arise between spouses can be traced to poor listening habits, which lead to misunderstanding, which in turn, can lead to a breakdown in communications. Confusion, tension, and defensiveness result and the stage is set for conflict and the possibility of a rapidly deteriorating relationship. The converse, of course, is also true. In a quality marriage, poor listening habits are kept to a minimum.

Rod and Sarah are poor listeners. They divorced approximately a year ago. Rod went his way, bitter, resentful, defeated, while Sarah remained in the house with their infant son, completely confused, outraged, hurt, and embarrassed about what she saw as the sudden breakdown of their marriage.

To hear Rod tell it, it was far from sudden. It began, according to him, soon after they were married, when he gradually began to realize his young bride was anything but an effective listener. Try as he may, he could not get through to her on so many occasions. Like the time he needed to tell her about his utter disappointment at the so-called tremendous job opportunity he accepted only to find it a real wash-out, and how badly he wanted to quit and try elsewhere!

Sarah threw him what I call the *brick wall technique*, one of the most devastating and humiliating forms of poor listening.[3] It's non-listening at its worst. Every time he attempted to explain his position, she immediately left the room with the angry retort that he made his bed, now sleep in it. With her pregnant, this was no time to think of looking for another job! Rod became a very lonely man very quickly. Eventually he stopped trying to confide in his wife and sought empathy elsewhere.

I am not suggesting that every time a spouse wants to speak, the partner should drop everything and listen. There are any number of occasions when, due to the press of the moment, effective listening is out of the question. The point is that when such a situation arises, you can make a "date" to get together as soon as possible, and discuss whatever has to be aired. Sarah simply refused to hear Rod out. She had no time for his immediate need.

Another poor listening habit involves what I refer to as the *trance technique*. A manager was quite adept at using this technique on subordinates he found quite boring and unexciting. Joe, for example, would come to his office to report on a particular problem that the manager felt he already knew all about. However, he did not want to hurt Joe's feelings by putting off his monologue, so he would sit up straight, lean forward a bit, fix his eyes on Joe, not move a muscle of his body, and pretend he was listening! In reality he was miles away in his own biocomputer, thinking of other matters.

He experienced quite a lesson some time later. He faked listening once too often. He apparently did not hear one of his staff tell him of a very serious problem that required him to make a management decision within twenty-four hours. The decision, of course, was not forthcoming, and he was hard put to explain his failure to do so to the vice president of marketing. Unfortunately, it cost him a much desired promotion.

This trance technique is certainly less apt to get you into trouble if you decide to use it in a social setting, i.e., a cocktail party where everyone is talking at once anyhow. But to resort to this kind of one-way communication when the speaker is trying to provide what he or she considers important is to set up the potential for misunderstanding and confusion. Many a marital conflict has arisen because one partner was faking listening to the other and misunderstanding and confusion resulted.

I have witnessed this on any number of occasions. The husband, for instance, is attempting to explain the reason or reasons behind some particular behavior that his wife finds unacceptable. She is staring straight at him, her body still and fixed as though she were absorbing his every word. When he finishes, I surprise her by asking her to feed back what he just said, and she is unable to do so! She has been inside herself (which is what a trance is) and heard nothing he said. Had I not asked for feedback, both would have been entirely oblivious of the fact that there hadn't been any communication. Imagine what chaos that would have led to!

There is another poor listening habit that is not unique to the marital situation, but is surely used more frequently in this context than any other, the *conversion technique.*

Maureen comes home from a rough day at the office, and really needs an empathic ear to listen to her. She wants ever so badly to talk to her husband about how hurt she is, how used and put down she feels. So she does, only to find that Jack, although he means well, refuses to enter her world. Instead of playing counselor (an appropriate posture in a situation like this) and allowing his wife to express her feelings and spill her guts, so to speak, he listens intently only until he feels he knows what's up; then he tries to *convert* Maureen to his way of thinking and feeling about the incident.

Maureen says she doesn't understand why her boss chose Alice to cover the president's talk when he knows very well Alice is woefully inexperienced in the political arena, while she has an excellent journalistic track record in handling public officials. Besides, she has broken her neck in the last two years helping to put the paper back on its feet and make it a force again. Now she really is beginning to think she has been used, and people like Alice, because they are younger, are groomed to take over.

Wanting to help, Jack jumps in at this point and attempts to convert her. He tells her she shouldn't feel the way she does. Then he tells her she ought to accept the fact that there is no love lost in business, that no matter what business you are in, there comes a time when you begin to feel the younger employee breathing down your neck. Either you acknowledge that as part of the competitive game and rise to the occasion, or you get out. Finally, he gently but firmly admonishes her for her lack of perspective and warns her that if she intends to remain with the newspaper, she must learn to roll with the punches.

When Jack finishes, he secretly feels pretty good about what he had to say. In fact, he remarks to his wife that this is the sort of healthy dialogue they should have more often. Maureen does not want to hurt her well-meaning husband and weakly affirms his evaluation and secretly wishes she had someone near she could really open up to. She wants to ventilate, not be given a pep talk intended to convert her to her husband's way of thinking!

I have a friend who is a genuine giver, the epitome of generosity. And yet I find it so difficult to converse with her because she is also the epitome of yet another poor listening habit, perhaps the most common of all, the *blocker technique*. In short, she blocks the flow of conversation by constantly interrupting the speaker, either by completing the expression of thought, or by jumping in with a deluge of questions to a point where the dialogue deteriorates into a question-answer scenario, if it goes that far. What usually happens is that everyone closes down and she is left to do the talking. Her husband has developed a strategy for handling this. He talks very little. And she wonders why!

In my counseling office there is a couple seated across from me. She is speaking to her husband and to me, trying to explain her reaction to a specific situation that occurred during the week. Her husband is looking in her direction as she speaks, but his eyes are actually focused on a spot above and to the right of her head. He seems to be looking at something on the wall behind her, perhaps the painting.

I also notice him lightly tapping his fingers on the arm of the chair, while partially covering his mouth with his other hand. Once in a while he almost imperceptibly glances toward the wall clock to his right, then adjusts his body position and squints his eyes as he wrinkles his forehead and his eyes go up for a split second.

She stops, looks at him with tears in her eyes, turns to me and speaks with an air of defeat and resignation: "What's the use. He never listens to me anyhow." He reacts instantly, "What the hell are you talking about! I haven't said a word in ten minutes!" She is ready for him. "You're right, George. You haven't said a word, because you haven't been here for ten minutes! In fact, you haven't been here since we got married!"

George is completely and honestly befuddled. He really has no idea where Cindy is coming from. He is unaware that he has closed her off through his body language, which said to her, "When are you going to finish so I can tell the counselor what happened last Wednesday?"

The physical (observable) behaviors George exhibited signaled to Cindy, consciously or unconsciously, that her message was falling upon at least partially deaf ears. As far as she was concerned, his body language revealed his inattentiveness.

Body language has a great deal to do with effective listening, or the lack of it. George, unfortunately, gave a splendid demonstration of one-ear-on-a-stick technique for poor listening. He thought he was listening, but his body said otherwise! And Cindy knew it...so did I!

Sigmund Freud is one of my heroes. This is why I have named this particular poor listening habit after him, the *Sigmund Freud technique* for turning people off who are trying to tell it as they see it. It works like this. Hans is speaking to Gert about a specific issue in his life that he is obviously puzzled about. Gert listens very attentively until Hans has fairly well exhausted his subject. Gert then (in fantasy) places Hans upon a couch and proceeds to analyze and interpret what Hans was saying! She explains to him what is really troubling him, why it's troubling him, and what he should do about it. I know of no better way to help a person feel like a real fool than to drop a chunk of psychoanalysis in his lap. But how often we do it!

Sigmund Freud is considered the father of psychoanalysis. He developed a theory and technique of psychoanalysis that evidently worked quite effectively in his office. Married couples ought to leave it there!

One final thought on the matter of poor listening habits in marriage. This may confuse some readers: The misuse of silence while listening can be devastating to a relationship! Put simply, we can abuse the skill of silence while someone is speaking by failing to respond verbally or non-verbally. A gentleman nearly went out of his mind trying to get his wife to respond when they were having a difference of opinion. His attempts to discuss their differences only met with what he called her deadpan expression, and he ended up more often than not in an angry and impotent monologue with himself.

There is a time for silence, and there is a time for reflection and feedback. The effective listener knows the difference. Evidently, his wife did not. She was under the impression that if she "kept her mouth shut," as she later put it, there would be less chance of an argument, something she had always dreaded from the time she was a child when her parents use to fight at the drop of a hat. I can well understand her hesitancy to argue under these circumstances, but refusing to speak up at all and risk an interchange in favor of settling a conflict compatibly seems to be severely self-defeating in the long run.

Couples growing quality marriages are aware of these poor listening habits and consciously strive to avoid them as much as possible. Avoiding poor listening habits, however, is only one side of the coin. The other side has to do with the positive: what spouses do that makes them effective listeners.

Being an effective listener involves two variables: one, a set of attitudes; the other, a set of behaviors and skills. Husbands and wives who are effective listeners possess these attitudes and skills to an admirable degree.

I define an attitude as a mental position or feeling regarding a fact or state. A person's attitude toward someone or something is internal and can only be recognized by another through the way that person acts or behaves. If, for example, I say Mr. Richardson is very loving toward his wife, I am indicating his attitude, which I have come to recognize by observing the way he behaves toward her over a period of time. In terms of effective listening, there are several distinct, yet related, attitudes that husbands and wives with satisfying and lasting marriages possess.

The first attitude is a desire to step into the other's shoes. Authorities in the field of human communications frequently refer to this attitude as empathy. A person is an empathic listener who wants to truly understand what the speaker is thinking or feeling at the moment. She desires to experience as best she can the internal experience of the other. This is an especially important attitude to have if you are sincerely interested in avoiding misunderstanding and misinterpretation in communication with your spouse...or anyone for that matter.

Another attitude that promotes effective listening among partners is the belief that each person really creates his own world. This attitude is difficult for many people to grasp. In essence, each of us is the final judge or decision maker as to what is real, what is true, what is right in our environment. That is why two people can be exposed to the same situation, yet react quite differently. No two people actually see the same rose in an identical manner.

What this means is that the wife or husband who is an effective listener believes the speaker has the right to think, feel, and speak from her or his own perspective. She may not agree with his evaluation of a situation, but she can understand how and why he reacts the way he does.

A third attitude that couples in quality marriages manifest is their need to bridge the I-Thou gap! This attitude is the key to their ability to synergize their relationships. They are convinced that although each human being is an individual in the truest sense of the word, still, "no man is an island." We need each other, we are dependent upon each other; we are one, for as someone once said, "When one tugs at a single thing in nature, he finds it attached to the rest of the world."

Couples in quality marriages know there is no more powerful tool for relieving the stress and anxiety of aloneness, for bridging the gap between the I and the Thou, for maintaining loving contact with one another than the art of effective listening. It is this communication still more than anything else that supports and enhances the us-ness in marriage.

Spouses who are effective listeners not only possess these attitudes, but also exhibit a more or less common set of behaviors when listening to each other that reflect these attitudes.

Ray and Sue are effective listeners. They really put their ears on a stick when communicating with each other. If you were to observe what they do, you would notice these behaviors:

*Rapport Behaviors.* Ray and Sue are having dinner at their favorite restaurant. They are seated across from each other at a small table in the center of the room. Sue is speaking. Notice what Ray is doing. You may respond at first, "He is doing nothing." On the contrary, he is doing a great deal. Ray is silent as Sue speaks. He maintains eye contact with her, nods his head ever so slightly on occasion, and leans just a bit forward, his arms loosely crossed and resting lightly on the edge of the table in front of him.

By his posture, his non-verbal body language, he is conveying the idea that he is in rapport with her and is attentive to what she is saying. Notice something else, quite significant too. Look under the table and watch how his feet move in sync with her foot movements. How can he know to do that? He can't, consciously!

Unconsciously, however, he is matching and pacing her body movements, pretty good proof that they are in rapport, and that excellent communication is going on at the moment. If you could see their facial expressions, e.g., lifting of the eyebrows simultaneously, you would also observe that he is actually mirroring her expressions ever so slightly. She smiles, he smiles. She squints her eyebrows at one point, he does also.

He is not playing games; he isn't even aware he is doing this mirroring. And even if he were, that would be just fine because we have discovered that people who listen effectively establish and maintain rapport through such non-verbal behavior, whether they are conscious of doing it or not. What Ray's non-verbal behavior and attentive silence are saying to Sue is, "Hey, darling, you have something to say, and I am listening to you!" That has to make Sue feel accepted.

*Leading Behaviors.* Of course, Ray is not going to fall into the trap of overdoing silence (abusing listening, as I discussed earlier). If you put your own ears on a stick, you will hear him casually leading Sue with verbal expressions of interest, therefore breaking his silence from time to time with such expressions as; "Uh huh," "Yes," "Right," "I hear you," "Go on." These are leading cues in that they simply encourage Sue to continue speaking.

The important thing is that they are non-evaluative or non-judgmental. That is, they say nothing about how Ray evaluates what she is saying. In effect, he has internally suspended judgment for the moment, and just wants her to say what she has to say, so he leads her. This is what most psychotherapists do very well when trying to obtain needed information from a client. They lead them to continue to speak through their "hums" and "uh huhs."

*Questioning Behaviors.* An effective listener knows how to ask questions, and more importantly, he knows why he is asking the questions he does! Ray is a good questioner. There are only two reasons he questions Sue. Either he asks her a question because he needs more information in order to better understand her, or he asks because he feels his question will prompt her to think through her concern in more detail. Hopefully, this will help her to get a better feel for what she is trying to sort through.

The first thing to notice is that he doesn't ask too many questions. Frequency of questions can often distract people from what they are really trying to think through and verbalize. I'm sure you've had this experience. You are attempting to think through something by talking about it, and someone keeps interrupting with a flood of questions! More often than not, the person doesn't even wait for your answer, but goes right on to the next question while you're trying to respond. Talk about a stressful conversation!

Another thing to notice is that Ray rarely asks Sue why. "Why" questions will drive people to drink, and in the long run they are probably the most useless and unproductive way to ask a question. Yet, we husbands and wives persist in bombarding each other and especially our children with why questions. About the only thing a why question does is force a person to rationalize an answer that will satisfy the questioner. Usually the questioner isn't satisfied anyhow.

Take this ridiculous scenario as an example. Little Johnnie Smallchild is sitting at the dinner table and reaches for a piece of bread, knocking over his glass of milk in the process. The glass falls to the floor and breaks, and the tablecloth and carpet are saturated with the milk. Dad angrily asks, "Why did you do that?" Teary eyed and frightened, Johnnie must instantly access his little biocomputer and immediately find an answer to dad's question that will save him from his father's wrath.

"I wanted a piece of bread, and the glass was in my way," he replies, knowing deep in his heart his reason will hold little weight, if any, in his parent's mind. He is correct. Dad ignores his son's response and directs another useless query at him. "So why didn't you watch what you were doing?" Now that is a really tough one. How do you answer that one to dad's satisfaction? You don't, of course, and the useless interrogation goes on until Mom steps in and calls it a draw.

How much more profitable for all concerned had dad questioned his son along these lines. "OK, Johnnie, how do you think you can prevent this sort of accident from happening again?"

I always find myself squirming when husbands and wives in counseling begin to throw the why questions at each other. It is usually a sign of getting nowhere fast! I am not advocating we banish the why question. There are occasions when it is most appropriate. In the field of diagnostic medicine, for instance, asking why such symptoms occur is quite suitable and, we hope, most advantageous in terms of the treatment. As for human behavior, however, a why question is often useless because no answer is satisfactory. If you challenge this statement, stop and think. When it comes to determining the reason for a person's behavior, there is no limit to the number of reasons he or she will do something, so it is useless to attempt to sort them out and list them.

Why, for example, did Herb arrive home at 11:30 P.M. Friday after promising Hildie he would only have one drink with his co-workers to celebrate the successful completion of the department's Fairlane Project?

A very agitated Hildie asked why when Herb finally arrived home. First he explained to her that his boss showed up at the party, so he felt he should hang around a bit longer. He didn't want Sam to think he didn't care about the project's happy ending. Hildie was not satisfied, so she asked another why. Herb responded that he had tried to call her but the line was busy for over an hour. Undaunted in her quest for the truth, Hildie again hit Herb with a why; to which Herb, his patience now rapidly deteriorating, replied that he does indeed think of Hildie and the kids, and that the fact he came home later than either one of them anticipated is no indication that he has lost interest in her and the children.

Still very dissatisfied with Herb's answers, Hildie then switched gears and moved into a series of should statements, beginning with, "You should know by now that I get upset when you're not home at the time you say you will be home." Etc.

Why questions always lead to should statements. When one person begins to "should" all over another, the latter inevitably begins to ask why questions, followed by should statements— and the argument goes on!

Ray is ready to admit that early in his relationship with Sue he favored the why-should approach to communicating with his wife. When she let him know in no uncertain terms how put down she always felt when he did this, he ceased and desisted, and both began to examine their communication behaviors more closely, with mutually satisfying results.

*Feedback Behaviors.*   Spouses who are good listeners are very adept at reflecting what their partners are saying. They play back to their husbands and wives what they heard them say, or rather what they thought they heard them say.

Sue is equally as effective as Ray when it comes to listening. She is a real natural at feeding back. She does this, as she says, because her dad modeled this specific communication behavior quite effectively as she was growing up. Consequently, while she and Ray certainly have their misunderstandings from time to time, the incidents of misunderstanding and misinterpretation are kept to an impressive minimum.

Quite simply put, as Ray is speaking, Sue will reflect to him what she understands him to be saying. If she is accurate, he will agree and continue to express his thoughts. If she is off the mark, he will repeat his thought until she has grasped the meaning of his message.

It is easy to realize why they have few arguments that are precipitated by misunderstanding, the root cause of all conjugal conflict. They have their disagreements, but they usually know where each other is coming from through their mutual efforts to provide feedback. They may not always agree on a particular issue, but they understand each other's perspective, and that is the beginning of the compatible resolution of differences in marriage for anyone.

Feeding back what you think another means by what he or she is saying is one aspect of listening effectively. Feeding back or reflecting what another is feeling while speaking is yet another aspect, one that is vital to building and maintaining rapport in a relationship. We all know how good we feel when someone shows us empathy. Empathy is nothing more than picking up the feelings of another accurately and reflecting them back. "Wow, she actually understands how I feel!" is a wonderful experience.

Being able and willing to put your ears on a stick is a characteristic of men and women living quality relationships.

## CHAPTER ELEVEN

# Put Your Cards on the Table

Quality relationships demand not only effective listening, but equally effective openness and honesty on the part of husbands and wives. Couples should "put their cards on the table" when occasions arise that call for healthy and honest confrontation and self-assertion. What is of interest here is that these men and women know when and how to level, so that ordinarily there is very little serious disruption to their relationship when a disagreement occurs. With spouses less skilled in the art of conjugal persuasion, disruption of the relationship may more often take place.

These people are not manipulators or controllers, attempting to trick their partners into submission or change of one kind or another. Rather, they are open, honest, and transparent in their dialogue. They are flexible in their beliefs and values, yet emphatically assertive when necessary. They invite attention because they speak a language of genuine concern and care-filled persuasion.

When to confront or assert oneself is of significant importance in any relationship. "To assert or not to assert" is the question. Not too many years ago, sundry participants attending assertiveness training workshops came away from their enlightening weekends convinced they had to confront friend and foe alike at the drop of a hat in reaction to any behavior they found unacceptable. Assertiveness became the much sought after virtue, while timidity and reticence became social no-nos.

From what I observed during those times, many marriages were harmed because well-meaning husbands and wives overreacted to the gospel of confrontation as preached by scores of equally well-meaning zealots of assertiveness. Spouses found themselves in conflict over issues best handled by way of *self-modification* or *environmental modification* rather than demands for forced change through confrontation.

Self-modification is another name for flip-flopping (Chapter Nine). Environmental modification is something I frequently recommend to parents who are forever upset about the manner in which their children keep their bedrooms. Rather than continually getting your knees in a knot, why not simply close the door? Many times it is much easier to modify a situation (like closing a door) than to insist on someone changing!

For years, Bill tried in vain to persuade Janice to have their evening meal prepared by five-thirty, so he could eat in a leisurely manner before going to work. Try as she might, Janice invariably got caught up in other affairs, and the meal, three out of five times, would be put on the table late, forcing Bill to forego the pleasure of a relaxed dinner. While walking the mall one weekend, he saw in an appliance store window the answer to his prayer, a microwave oven! Bill modified his environment immediately, and Janice, after some weak attempts to appear insulted, gladly accepted her husband's solution.

Self-modification and environmental modification are options available to quality marriage partners. These choices reduce but don't eliminate the need to confront each other in a more or less stressful effort to initiate some behavioral change.

When to assert oneself in marriage? When to confront one's

spouse and level? When to put one's cards on the table and risk it? As infrequently as possible. In those relationships that are mutually satisfying and lasting, spouses generally confront as a last resort. If they can modify or reframe their own thinking about a disturbing issue and become neutral, if not comfortable, with things as they are, they are more likely to do so rather than confront. If they can modify the environment and thereby resolve the issue, they are more likely to do so.

However, in the event that either or both of these strategies prove unacceptable to them, then they will level with their spouse in the hope that direct confrontation will move the other to make whatever adjustment is needed, or at least open the door for win-win negotiations.

One thing they will not do, at least not consciously for any length of time, is subject themselves to psychic constipation (Chapter Five). Holding things in or gunnysacking with any degree of frequency is what moody people do. I have yet to come upon a moody spouse involved in a quality marriage; moody people and quality relationships just don't go together.

Treading water in favor of a more appropriate time to confront is not, however, gunnysacking, nor is it indicative of moodiness. Knowing the lay of the land, sensing the most propitious moment to level with one's partner, is a *sine qua non* for effective confrontation. Unfortunately, too often a harried husband or wife plunges in before testing the waters, only to find an icy response to his or her honest, though ill-timed, effort to be forthright and honest.

Sometimes at a seminar people decidedly disagree with my caution to confront as a last resort. There are those in the audience who feel that if a husband and wife truly love each other, they should feel free enough to level any time they have a need to, regardless of the issue involved or the circumstances at the moment. As one young woman put it, "If I can't be transparent and open with my husband, then what is this thing called marital love?"

Ideally, I suppose, it would be fantastic were married mortals at a point in human evolution where love for self and one another eliminated the hurt, anger, embarrassment, rejection, etc., they frequently feel when spouses level about something they do or say that they find objectionable. But this is not the case. Try as we may, if indeed we try to soften the blow, all too often feelings are hurt, tempers flair, battle lines are drawn, and the fight is on! Sooner or later the dust settles, and each goes off to tend his or her wounds, wondering if it's all worth it. No one really wins, least of all the relationship.

So often this is because of the lack of timing and know-how. People growing quality marriages confront each other, no question about it. They also often feel pain when confronted, no question about it, but they have the timing and know-how to greatly reduce the pain and to get results acceptable to both. When and how are the key issues when putting your cards on the table.

Mick wanted very much to level with Terri about her work schedule. Three nights a week was too much, as far as he was concerned. They had two preschool children, and he felt they were being neglected. He had been treading water for a while because he knew that his wife was thrilled with her newly appointed position. Recently, however, he had begun to gunnysack; his resentment and opposition had grown to a point where he wanted to demand she either back off the night work or quit.

They were growing a quality marriage up till that time. Mick dearly wanted to continue to do so, but he was puzzled. What to do? He hesitated to confront Terri and insist she modify her hours, yet he knew he could not continue to tolerate the situation. He had reasoned with himself over and over to no avail. He had thought of alternative ways to satisfy both his need and that of his children. Again, all to no avail.

Finally, he decided to level with Terri. He almost confronted her one night when she was two hours late coming home from work. He was frantic about her safety, and the youngsters were driving him up a wall crying for their mother. Terri came in obviously washed out and on the verge of tears. Mick backed off, listened to her distress, and together they put the kids to bed. He waited till the following weekend, when they were away together and alone overnight at the shore, to confront his wife. It still wasn't easy to resolve the situation, but at least they were ahead of the game under those relaxing conditions, much better than attempting to discuss the problem that tense night. Timing is vital if you want the relationship to remain intact.

Knowing how to confront is equally important. In examining how to level or confront, quality marriage couples use (consciously or unconsciously) some of the following strategies.

*Attack the Problem, Not the Person.* I know of no better, quicker, or more certain method for blocking the very change one wants in another's behavior than verbally or non-verbally to denigrate that person's self-esteem and sense of personal worth by blaming, accusing, name calling, ridiculing, threatening, or preaching. Couples in trouble make frequent use of such tactics in futile efforts to change the spouse's behavior. How often in counseling sessions I witness such devastating dialogue.

Quality marriage couples, on the other hand, attack the problem, *not the person.* Not too long ago, I was visiting a married couple who suddenly found themselves in a hot and heavy argument, each trying to persuade the other to accept his or her point of view about a family issue. For a while I knew I did not even exist for them. They went toe to toe and nose to nose, their voices rising, as they attempted to outshout each other. The husband was so red in the face and neck, I began to fear. His wife, just as insistent and adamant as he was, matched him word for word. After some ten minutes, they began to exhaust themselves, and the tempo of the argument slackened noticeably.

I did not butt in to try to reconcile their differences. Instead, I paid close attention to how they were handling themselves. When they finally sank back in obvious frustration, and their silence began to echo about the living room, I smiled and quietly congratulated them for the way they went about their argument. With all their screaming and yelling, *they stuck to the issue and not once did they attack the other's person.*

They were truly amazed at my observations. They admitted, a bit sheepishly, that they were not consciously avoiding blaming or accusing each other, or name calling, ridiculing, or threatening each other. They just didn't do those kinds of things, even in the heat of an argument. They never thought to do it.

When I asked them where they were going to go with their argument, since neither looked like a winner at the moment, and no resolution was apparently forthcoming, they glanced at each other, laughed, and agreed that they'd work out a compatible solution some other time. And they did. They've been married now thirty-five years, thirty-five satisfying years according to them. Do they still argue? Is the pope Catholic?

Husbands and wives growing quality relationships are not immune to arguing. Nor are they immunized against attacking the person rather than the problem. What they have going for them in a big way, however, is the infrequency with which this sort of thing occurs; they are aware that they have to zero in on what they observe to be the disturbing behavior that, in their opinion, merits correction or adjustment. They focus upon what they see or hear, and that usually makes all the difference.

For example, Jeanne is fed up with her husband's manner of removing his socks when retiring for the night. She has reminded him repeatedly, to no avail, to turn them right side out and separate them before placing them in the hamper. Rolling them up in a ball and dropping them alongside the hamper is not her idea of thoughtfulness. She is tired of picking up after him.

She tries once again. "Gavin, you make me sick. You're about as considerate and sensitive a person as your mother! You don't give a tinker's damn about my feelings and the extra work you cause people. I never realized before we were married how lazy and careless you really are!"

Now if that is not attacking the person rather than the problem, what is? And each time she has confronted him, her message has been more or less the same. No wonder she hasn't gotten to first base, even though Gavin keeps telling her he'll try to remember. No one wants to feel put down, embarrassed, humiliated, or shamed. Some people seem to think, however, that a marriage certificate is a license to say whatever they please to their spouse. How ironic that so many husbands and wives would never dare even think of confronting another human being in such a respect-less fashion, but they do not hesitate to lay it on their partners. The unfortunate part is that in so many instances it is done without intent. People are just not aware. Quality marriage couples apparently are.

*Own Your Own World.* Two thousand years ago a Greek philosopher observed, "Men are not troubled by things themselves, but by their own thoughts and feelings about things." That statement is filled with wisdom, a wisdom our couples growing satisfying and lasting relationships seem to partake of, a wisdom that enables these husbands and wives to produce a bit of magic when they have the need to level with each other. It is a wisdom Jeanne failed to demonstrate when she confronted Gavin.

Jeanne began her confrontation by telling Gavin he made her sick. Imagine, he made her sick! Where did her feeling really come from? Who produced it and how? It came from the way she appraised the situation. In effect, it was generated by her own thought process. She saw the rolled-up socks next to the hamper. She took this scene and internalized it, evaluating it from her own belief system (values), which obviously dictated that one does not roll up one's socks into a ball and then drop them by the hamper. She then went another step and decided that her husband's behavior indicated he was as insensitive as his mother, etc.

From this mental process, Jeanne then developed a feeling within herself that she labeled "sick." Then she fell into a trap and took the feeling she had internally produced and accused Gavin of causing it. "Gavin, you make me sick!"

I know of no more effective way to encourage defensiveness and resistance on the part of one you are attempting to confront in the hope of promoting positive behavioral change than to accuse the person of causing the negative feelings you are experiencing. Regardless of the circumstances, no one enjoys being blamed for someone else's unhappiness. Believe it or not, words and the way we use them in constructive criticism make the difference between maintaining or even enhancing an intimate relationship, and hurting or even destroying it.

People are less apt to respond defensively or to counter-attack in the face of critical confrontations if you initially acknowledge responsibility for your own feelings, whatever they may be. Far better had Jeanne either ignored saying the piece about feeling sick, or phrased it in such a way that there would be no question as to the source of the feeling; e.g., "Gavin, I feel discounted when I see your socks...etc."

If you think this matter inconsequential, recall the last time someone treated you badly. In all honesty, what was your initial response? The elegant communicator pays close attention to the "small" things that really matter.

Couples in quality marriages are, for the most part, elegant communicators. When they put their cards on the table, they keep a couple of ideas in mind. For one thing, they remember that they are offering their partners constructive criticism because they hope for a behavioral change. Why, then, say something that might bring resistance rather than change? The other thing they remember is to speak in a manner that will provide small risk, if any, of their spouse feeling put down or the relationship being hurt. Since self-esteem is an important commodity for us, a crushed ego does not enhance a relationship.

A final point related to this issue is the matter of congruency of feeling when constructively criticizing your spouse. Frequently enough, this congruence in one's feelings is no easy task to master. It is to express one's feelings as one actually feels—no game playing or attempts at manipulation. It is telling it as you feel it in as transparent a manner as possible.

The problem, for one thing, is that we often experience a constellation of feelings in response to an event, and that can make it difficult to express what we are feeling, so we use words like confused, upset, angry, or mad.

Another reason we often find it difficult to be congruent and transparent in expressing our feelings is that we have been trained from childhood to suppress our negative feelings and emotions: "Big boys don't cry" and "Young ladies don't stamp their feet" (at least not publicly). The result is that we have learned to mask our feelings to a point where as adults we often honestly don't recognize what we really feel.

Take anger, for example. Anger is a smoke screen. The primary feeling behind anger is either hurt or fear. But how often we fail to probe the anger we are feeling and become aware of the hurt or fear behind it? Quite a bit, as far as I can see. Your efforts at confrontation are usually far more effective when you can verbalize the real pain of hurt or fear, rather than resort to the expression of anger as a smoke screen.

I'm certain Jeanne would have been much more successful had she been able to express the feeling of hurt she was experiencing. I recall an aquaintance of mine who was labeled an angry man by his employees always had a snarl on his face, never a smile. He really wasn't an angry man. He was a fear-filled retail store owner who was forever living in dread that his newly formed business would soon fail. His fear came across as perpetual anger. He even began to believe it, and that prompted him to seek counseling.

*Sell Your Reasons...Without the "Or Else."* This specific chunk of a healthy and effective confrontation actually piggybacks the chunk I've just discussed. Quality marriage couples rarely expect each other to mind read. "I am not only going to tell you how I feel, but I'm also going to tell you how I got to feel this way." In short, "I'm going to tell you my reasons for confronting you!" They take little for granted because they know it is close to a miracle that human beings are able to communicate in the first place. So they explain as clearly and as concisely as possible the reasons for their criticism. They try to express their convictions on the matter in an honest and sincere manner, trusting that their explanation will be accepted and change will result, something that Jeanne neglected to do. She never really told Gavin what his unacceptable behavior cost her. She took it for granted that he knew all along. He did not. He considered it no big deal to stoop over, pick up a few pairs of rolled-up socks, straighten them out, and throw them in the hamper. "So what was her beef?"

What he didn't know, because she did not tell him, was that his failure to comply with her wishes in this matter made her eventually question the regard with which he held her in general. The oft-repeated incident of rolled-up-socks-by-the-hamper became a test, of sorts, of the degree of respect she felt he had for her. In effect, the cost to her was a decided lowering of her own self-esteem. In questioning her husband's regard for her, she threw her own self-esteem into question!

You say she shouldn't have done that, but that is not the issue. It happened because she failed to communicate her reasons. When she finally did, a dramatic change took place in his behavior and their relationship.

A professional salesperson at a relationship seminar reacted with contagious enthusiasm to this idea of selling your reasons. He thought the parallel between marital confrontation and selling was insightful.[2]

> When I sell a product, I have to convince the prospective buyer that what I have to sell is worth buying. In order to do that, I have to believe in the product; I have to convey this belief, and I have to clearly define my reasons for so believing. Then it is up to him to decide whether or not my product is worth buying.
>
> So, too, when I am trying to persuade my wife to change some behavior I find unacceptable, I have to convince her, that is, sell her on the idea that the change is worthwhile and in the best interests of both of us. Since in selling, to successfully close the transaction, I have to establish and maintain rapport with the buyer, so must I do so when interacting with my wife. God forbid I should downgrade a prospective buyer by blaming or accusing or labeling him! I wouldn't get to first base with that approach. Neither will I with my wife if I use that approach.
>
> And, of course, it is utterly ridiculous even to imagine I can persuade a customer to buy by using the "or else" method. Salespeople attempt the old fashioned threat routine from time to time. "If you don't buy X product now, you'll live to regret it!" It never really works over the long haul. It may work once on a particular buyer, but that customer will never come back. Same thing

with my wife. Trying to convince her through the "or else" routine only does one thing...she digs in deeper, and there is *no sale*. A threat, in or out of the marital context, is a power play.

Need I say more?

*Announce the Good News.* Elegant communicators use a balanced approach when putting their cards on the table. The *One Minute Manager* encourages leaders to use this balanced approach when confronting someone. How does it work? Make sure you acknowledge your spouse's pluses before you address his or her minuses.

Should the confronter try to cushion the blow by offering praise as well as constructive criticism? Yes. No matter how diplomatic you may attempt to be in confronting your partner, there is always a good chance that some pain will be felt. Letting your husband or wife know in specific terms how you appreciate, love, and respect him or her, while offering constructive criticism that you judge is warranted, can go a long way for him or her to be more open to what you are saying.

If that sounds as if I am advocating that you should manipulate your partner by flattery so that he or she will surrender, you are right...and you are wrong! You are right in that my hope is that my positive stroking will further my cause, i.e., aid in convincing my spouse to make an adjustment in behavior. Wrong, if you think I am making up something nice about her or exaggerating something positive she has done in order to accomplish this. My praise is *genuine* and my praise is *specific*.

These two points are most important. If you are going to stroke your spouse, it must be for real; otherwise, the entire confrontation is a manipulative farce. The second point is to be specific in your praise. The best way to do this is to pinpoint a particular behavior or activity your partner engages in that pleases you, and announce the good news. For example, Jeanne might have begun her confrontation with Gavin by indicating how appreciative she always is about how he pitches in with the weekend housecleaning and laundry chores, then go on to cite her need for him to be more attentive to the socks/hamper matter.

*Keep It Hush-Hush.* This most important strategy in a quality marriage couple's approach to confrontation would seem to be obvious to most, yet it is so often violated. Unless there is an immediate and urgent need to criticize your spouse, never, never do so in a group setting. Constructive criticism ought to be handled in private. If you need to know why, recall the last time you were confronted in public. Unless you are a masochist, it is usually a very unpleasant experience—for all involved.

Knowing when and how to put your cards on the table has a great deal to do with the growth of quality marriages. Even if your partner refuses to "buy" your constructive criticism and becomes defensive or resistant, you have set the stage for a win-win resolution of your differences through compatible negotiations.

## CHAPTER TWELVE

# Put Your Pride in Your Pocket

Pride is a fascinating human trait. Too much of it can lead to blind and uncompromising arrogance; too little of it can cause undue self-condemnation and depreciation. The right amount makes for a well-balanced person, someone we think of as a modest sort who has his or her head on straight.

Modest people have a healthy mix of justifiable pride and tasteful humility, which is why they are effective leaders and negotiators. Couples in quality marriages are modest people. They negotiate their differences and solve their problems in a win-win fashion. This chapter discusses how they are able to put their "pride in their pocket," when such behavior is called for, and resolve their difficulties in a way that couples in troubled relationships cannot. There is a definite structure, certain steps, to their problem-solving methodology. More often than not, they are only vaguely aware of these steps; they just do it to resolve their differences in a way acceptable to both spouses.

*Isolating the Issue.* This is the most important of these steps. Upwards of ninety-five percent of a couple's time and effort will be spent on this initial step in their pursuit of a solution to their problem. To do this takes patience, honesty, humility, and a certain commitment to the problem-solving process. Too often in a couple's anxiety to resolve an issue, they rush ahead toward a solution before they have clearly defined and isolated what the problem (issue) actually is. Quality marriage couples do not rush ahead. They curb their anxiety and take the time to define and isolate the issue. They agree upon what is causing the problem before they try to resolve it.

First of all, they are willing to put their ears on a stick and their cards on the table and take the time to listen to each other attempt to identify what each considers to be the crux of the matter. Neither uses a power-play strategy to force the other to acknowledge his or her definition of the problem. Nor do they feign agreement in order to get on with the process. They stick it out until both honestly agree upon the problem definition.

Mel and Sally are a good example. They were at odds about what supposedly was a simple, easily identified problem. Mel wanted to buy a new pickup truck and Sally preferred a custom van. So why waste time trying to read into it. It was simple and clear: Each wanted a different type of vehicle. Get on with the solution.

Not so. After some discussion, not about what to do regarding their difference, but about what the difference actually was, they finally agreed that the crux of the matter was not which vehicle to buy, but rather who's the boss! That was the immediate issue, a far cry from where they started.

Suppose they had not taken the time to clarify the issue and just jumped into what each considered to be the solution: "We'll buy the truck because it will...." "No, we'll buy the van because it will...." Can you just imagine where they might have gone from there, all to no avail. They would be going around in circles simply because the real issue was never put on the table.

That did not happen in Mel and Sally's case, however. They isolated and identified the specific issue, then began to resolve

it. Through their willingness to listen attentively and empath-
ically and speak honestly and congruently (and take the time
to do so), their discussions led them to the gradual realization
that their individual choice of vehicle was actually a metaphor for their confusion about leadership behavior in the marriage. That was the issue at hand. That was what really had
to be resolved.

And what was at the core of the problem or conflict between
them? Mel had been feeling increasingly irritated and hurt over
Sally's recent take-over attitude. Ever since she started full
time as principal secretary with an HMO group, Mel noticed she
was making decisions without consulting him, like buying various household appliances, making dates for social engagements,
or telling him what had to be done around the house. It also
seemed to him that she was out much more than before in the
evenings, and he was stuck at home with the kids.

On the other hand, Sally was feeling increasing distress
from her efforts to handle her job responsibilities efficiently,
and at the same time be the effective wife and mother she
wanted to be. She had begun to resent Mel's laid-back attitude
and his constant questioning about why she had to do this or
that, or go here or there. She saw his behavior as an indication
that he was the boss, expecting and demanding too much of her.

Interesting, isn't it? Until they began to open up, using the
truck/van issue for starters, each felt that the other was controlling the relationship. Each felt used and abused, a second-
rate citizen at best. Each felt the other was trying to be the
boss. Initially there were some accusations and blame throwing
on each one's part, but that subsided very quickly for three reasons: (1) The quality of the relationship took priority over individual hurts; (2) they were able to pocket their pride; and (3)
they were empathic listeners and honest confronters, so they
were able to truly understand where each was coming from.

A major difference I have found between couples enjoying satisfying and lasting relationships and those in troubled marriages regarding this first step in problem solving is that the latter couples do not assign top priority to the relationship; they

insist they are right and the other partner is wrong; they are very poor listeners, and because of too much pride are arrogant confronters. Consequently, these spouses never get past the first step, and more often than not end up arguing continually about what the argument is about.

*Naming Possible Solutions.* Mel and Sally went on to the second step. They exchanged possible solutions. "What can we do about this particular issue in our relationship?" became the question to be answered, rather than, "What will it be, the truck or the van?"

If couples in troubled marriages, by some stroke of fate, do happen to find their way to this step, they usually botch up the works at this juncture by employing the hard sell approach with each other. Each decides upon a solution and proceeds to inundate the other with the reasons why *that* solution is correct, right, the best, the most sensible, the most reasonable. In the process they completely ignore or give merely passing recognition to their spouse's solution, thus indicating that any solution not in accord with theirs is absolute idiocy.

Quality marriage couples like Mel and Sally execute step two quite differently. They brainstorm possible solutions to begin with. They try to think of a variety of ways their issue can be resolved before deciding which one or ones would be the most suitable. They don't shoot each other's ideas down as soon as they are voiced. They are modest enough to accept the fact that their spouse may very well have some significant input to contribute. In effect, they refrain from evaluating or making a judgment at this point in the process. They know that at this point what is important is to exchange or generate as many possible solutions as they can, because the more data they have to work with, the better decision(s) they will make in the long run. A paucity of solutions is frequently the reason for poor decision making—whether in the marketplace or the home.

In step two you really have to put your pride in your pocket. The temptation to reject your spouse's suggestion can be almost overwhelming, especially if the anxiety level is high. Mel and Sally both readily admit that often you have to talk yourself into resisting the temptation to cut the other off. One thing to say to yourself, which helps very much, is, "Whatever solution we come up with, it is absolutely necessary that it be acceptable to both of us, otherwise it will not work for long. Better to try to let the other suggest as many as possible, so *we* can come up with an answer to our problem that will make us both winners."

In discussing step two with workshop participants, I sometimes find they think this step is laborious, time consuming, and irritatingly mechanical and unnatural. My response is, "Yes, depending upon the circumstances, it can be laborious and time consuming, and possibly irritatingly mechanical and unnatural. But then, what is the alternative?" In most cases, what I am describing in some detail actually takes place rather rapidly. Mel and Sally spent little time on step two because they did such a good job on the prior step, isolating the issue. That often happens. Step two and the steps following frequently flow quite naturally and easily because step one was done carefully. Of course, if step one is done in a vague and confusing manner, it will be hard to come up with relevant, possible solutions.

Mel's list of possible solutions included the following: They should be more open and honest with their feelings about who is the boss when something happens that makes one of them feel put down; they should both become more aware of the fact that there are situations when one of them naturally becomes the leader and the other the follower (the give and take of marital management); he should become more active in the day-to-day decision-making process, rather than take a back seat and then complain about not being consulted; Sally should reduce the time she spends away from the family in the evening during the week; Sally should realize that he is the principal provider and think of curtailing her work schedule; Sally should be more understanding of the pressures he experiences in his work environment; etc.

Sally had her list, which included the first two of Mel's suggestions plus: She should be more aware of her husband's traditional blue collar background (not meant in any derogatory sense whatsoever); he should look for another job because it was obvious to her he needed more of a challenge in life—he was bored; he should take more of an interest in some avocation or hobby to occupy his time; she should consult him more often on the day-to-day matters of family living; etc.

*Choosing a Solution.* Once they had their solutions out on the table, they moved to the third step, choosing a solution(s). This involves two actions: evaluating the relative merits of the various proposed solutions, and choosing a mutually acceptable solution(s).

What criteria a couple uses to evaluate their solutions is highly individual in most cases. What is appropriate and meaningful to one couple in their specific context may not be so for another husband and wife. Mel and Sally, for example, decided that for a possible solution to be mutually acceptable, it had to insure that neither one would be made to feel like a second-class citizen in the home, and flexibility of leadership would be the order of the day in those instances where conjoint decision making was inappropriate.

As they discussed the pros and cons of various proposed solutions, they kept two things in mind. The first had to do with the tactic of persuasion. Each, at different times, attempted to sell the other on certain of the possible solutions. But it was a soft sell—no pushing, pressuring, demanding, threatening, manipulating allowed. Trying to influence or persuade the other through reasoning, presentation of facts and benefits, etc., was perfectly acceptable. In other words, each could comfortably say no to any of the solutions.

The second thing they kept in mind flowed logically from the first; namely, that for a solution to be chosen, both Mel and Sally had to agree on it. If only one of them found a particular solution acceptable and the other did not, then that solution was dumped. For instance, Sally's suggestion that her husband take up an avocation or hobby to occupy his time was unacceptable to Mel. He felt his jogging was sufficient, and he had no interest in taking up something in addition. Sally, on the other hand, did not accept Mel's idea that she curtail her work schedule and cut back on her full-time position at the office, although she did agree that her social calendar needed revision downward.

As frequently happens when a couple sincerely uses this step-by-step approach to problem solving, a certain synergy begins to take place and an elegant solution neither one had thought of previously gradually evolves from their discussions, usually a solution that is pretty much a combination of those the couple listed.

This synergism took place in Mel and Sally's case. They kept looking at their lists (which they had taken the time to write down) and discussing the pros and cons when it gradually dawned on each one that they were doing the very thing they were hoping to achieve. In effect, they were involved in conjoint leadership at the time, attempting to make decisions together that would be acceptable to both and benefit all in the family. In doing what they were doing, they had already taken step four.

*Doing It.* This final step would seem so obvious if one were following this step-by-step approach to problem solving. However, this is not always the case. It often happens that a couple (quality marriage or not) resolves to do something to alleviate their conflict, yet never get around to doing it. As a matter of fact, most marital discord is caused by this condition. A couple knows what the problem is; they know what has to be done; and they do nothing!

The inertia people experience when it is time to work at their marriage is appalling. They seem quite willing to expend time, effort, and money to resolve other problems in life, but when it comes to implementing a solution to a conjugal conflict, they often fail to do so. If couples in troubled marriages were willing to carry out even a third of the intelligent solutions they honestly know will greatly help their relationships, they would be well on their way to quality marriages.

Couples like Mel and Sally who follow through the problem-solving process by executing step four may find later on that their solution, when put into action, is not the answer or perhaps not the complete answer. Does that mean they failed? No. What it does mean is that they must go back to the drawing board and come up with a more effective solution.

Sometimes people get discouraged at their failure to effectively resolve a problem, especially if great amounts of time and effort went into the problem-solving process. This is understandable, particularly in America where people have been conditioned to cast their decisions in concrete and expect the results to be successful and unchangeable.

I prefer the Eastern mentality in this regard. It views all life as being in process. There are really no end events, and every decision is merely a benchmark in this process, subject to eventual change and adjustment, if only because there are so many variables in life that we are unable to take into account when we make a decision. We can't control our total environment, and many variables will impact our decisions, no matter what we try.

In essence, then, I might say that a couple enjoying a quality marriage may at first feel discouraged and disgruntled at their seeming failure to resolve a conflict, but they eventually shrug it off and go in search of yet another way to tackle the problem, knowing full well that marriage, like life, is a process without a lasting end event.

Mel and Sally still struggle at times with the problem of who's in charge, but they readily confess their conflicts in this regard are few and far between and much easier to handle when they do occur. Sally recently mentioned that they would "probably go to our graves with this issue still not completely resolved, if only because both of us are actually very good managers and effective leaders; so there is a natural tendency to want to take charge. We have to fight with ourselves at times to put our pride in our pockets and let the other do his thing."

Trading off leadership roles is no easy matter in the lives of many couples with whom I've worked. There are a great many strong-minded, competent, forceful personalities, husbands and wives, who know they have the capability to lead, and want to, and do. In my experience, a good deal of marital discord has to do with this issue of leadership in marriage: Who follows whom? Many of the more superficial issues are simply a smoke screen hiding this deeper issue.

Quality marriage couples do two things to handle this common problem. The first I've just discussed in some detail. They pocket their pride and use the four step problem-solving structure that Mel and Sally use from time to time. The second has to do with what I call leadership flexibility, and it too requires partners to put their pride in their pocket from time to time, and let the other take the lead.

There was a time in the history of marriage when the leader of the household and chief manager was considered to be the husband, who was also the breadwinner, provider, protector, and anything else that supported his role as C.E.O. "Father knows best," and "as long as I'm putting the bread on the table, you'll...." were common slogans of yesteryear. Actually, in many households, these slogans are still quite popular and well attended to today. However, some things are changing in society, and leadership flexibility in marriage is one of those changes gradually taking place, not as rapidly as many would like, but nevertheless happening.

What does leadership mean? In business and industry, it is generally defined as "the process of influencing the activities of an individual or a group in efforts toward goal achievement in a given situation."[1] Furthermore, "influencing" takes place in several different situations or a combination thereof. The leader may influence by reason of authority, by reason of superior knowledge and know-how, by reason of strength of personality, by reason of communication skills, etc.

This definition can and should be applied to marriage. Leadership in marriage is essentially no different than leadership in any other organization, with one obvious exception. Neither husband nor wife can legitimately try to lead by reason of his or her authority position, unless the other freely consents to this situation. I am not even sure, however, that Edith Bunker really consented to Archie's humorous yet painful tyranny!

In the world of business and industry, there is management

and leadership by reason of authority position, and it works. In troubled marriages, there is usually the attempt to manipulate, coerce, or persuade by reason of a self-appointed authority position; it rarely works.

Tom was adamant about his self-appointed authority position. At the time I met him and his wife, Mary Ellen, he had a very good salary in the computer industry, and they had been married two years. He knew what he wanted and how to get it. He was also convinced he knew what was best for his wife and their newborn daughter.

From the beginning of their relationship, as Mary Ellen tells it, Tom was a take-charge person who insisted on making the decisions with little or no input from her—or anyone else, for that matter. At first, she confesses, she felt rather proud of her husband and secure in his abiliiy and willingness to manage their young household. However, her enthusiasm wore thin rather quickly and the trouble began. There was no convincing him that she, too, had a right and need to share leadership and the decision-making responsibilities in the family.

About the time he began to white glove the results of her housekeeping chores, she reached out for professional help. She finally risked making a decision on her own and followed through with it. She entered counseling and insisted Tom join her. Fortunately, he got the message, and they are presently attempting to straighten out their leadership problem.

It hasn't been easy. Tom comes from a background that supported male dominance in the family, a caring and concerned dominance, but nevertheless, one that was also smothering and oppressive in many instances. There is progress, however, and I suspect this couple is starting to grow a quality marriage.

In quality marriages, the self-appointed authority position is minimally present. Leadership is shared and is flexible. Husbands and wives trade off leadership depending upon the particular situation, or they make decisions together when a specific context calls for conjoint management. They try to influence and persuade each other toward the achievement of some objective through their knowledge, know-how, personality traits, communication skills, etc., not because of some mythical or traditional authority position.

Spouses in quality relationships possess leadership flexibility because they are basically modest people and know when and how to pocket their pride and follow. And because they are modest people, they also know when and how to take the lead in the best interests of the relationship.

How, then, does a person cultivate this virtue of modesty in marriage? There are several ways quality couples do it:

1. Respect the knowledge, know-how, and experience of your partner, as well as yourself.
2. Listen attentively to his or her view of the matter, as well as your own.
3. Acknowledge that in the decision-making process, two heads are better than one.
4. When in doubt, trust your partner and risk following his or her suggestion.
5. When your partner fails in his or her leading efforts, be empathic in your criticism.

## CHAPTER THIRTEEN

# Touch and Go

Several months after her husband was killed in an automobile accident and she was left a single parent with four young children, Mary Beth came to see me. She was a distraught and grieving widow who, in spite of much family support, was finding it next to impossible to cope with her sudden loss and the prospect of raising her children alone.

In the course of our counseling, Mary Beth gradually revealed the full scope of her loving relationship with her deceased husband. They had been married twelve years and it was apparent they were growing a quality marriage. There was one particular detail she repeated quite often, his physical attentiveness to her. As she so descriptively put it, "His bag of kisses, hugs, and touches was never empty. He was the most demonstrative husband and father who ever lived. There was no way I could stay angry with him. He'd see I was bent out of shape, and with that huge Irish grin of his, he would come to me, and before I could even make believe I wanted to resist, he'd hug me right off my feet, plant a kiss on my lips, set me down with a laugh, and out the kitchen door he'd go. I began to call it his 'touch and go' routine. And it worked...most of the time."

Recently a client was seriously considering a divorce from her husband after twenty-seven years of marriage. Among her reasons was one she considered to be the most painfully disappointing of all. In all their years together "he rarely, if ever, shows me any affection except when he wants sex; and then it's the slam, bam, thank you ma'am sort of love making."

She went on to explain that time and again she pleaded with him to show her attention and affection apart from sexual relations. She wanted to be kissed, hugged, to be caressed, to be touched and fondled. His response was that he couldn't be so demonstrative because his parents had never been, and besides, he showed his love in other ways (e.g., working about the house, making a good living). She claimed he behaved no differently toward her than he did his friends when it came to demonstrations of attentiveness and affection. She lived with him, and yet felt very isolated from him.

Her husband came to see me at my request, and I gently approached the issue. He acknowledged the problem, briefly repeated what she had told me about his upbringing, and then attempted to reduce the significance of the issue with the observation, "She brings this up from time to time. I don't see that it's any big deal. But you know women are like that. They need constant reassurance we still love them. Thank goodness men are different, or I'd have a heck of a time with my staff."

I quietly countered by quickly relating the story of Tom and Margot. Tom was a professional athlete. He "dragged" Margot into my office because he was fed up with her lack of affection toward him. In his words, "She was great in bed once she got going, but getting a kiss or a hug in the kitchen was like pulling teeth."

Coming from a giant of a man who played a sport that earned him a very enviable income and the adulation of many fans, this seemed a bit amusing until I quickly discovered how sensitive a human being he was, and how much the hugs, kisses, and touches meant to him. To him, such physical contact signaled the intimacy and love he wanted between himself and his wife. Moral of the story: Men and women aren't so different!

Interesting sidelight, too. Tom needed this kind of affection and attention, as he revealed, because his parents never showed it at home! These are circumstances like those the gentleman to whom I was relating the story voiced in his own defense.

Hugs, kisses, caresses, touches, and other personal aphrodisiacs, that is what quality marriages are made of. Men and women in these kinds of relationships are usually well aware of the need to demonstrate loving intimacy, caring, concern, and exclusivity through physical contact, as well as verbal exchange.

My dad was a toucher and a hugger par excellence. In fact, when I met Tom and Margot, Tom reminded me of my father. Both were big physical men who were leaders, yet they were gentle, sensitive, empathic individuals. My dad modeled the use of non-verbal communication to show affection and attention in a manner that could not escape us children. With mother as well as with us, he constantly connected in so many different ways.

When he left for work, whoever was around got a kiss and bear hug that was repeated when he arrived home in the evening. Whenever any of us prepared to leave the house, God help us if we didn't make the rounds, kissing and hugging the family members who were present. Our neighborhood friends could never understand why we kissed our parents goodbye, even though we were only going out to play, or to school, or to the store.

A great regret of mine is that I was absent when my father died suddenly from a massive heart attack, a matter of a minute or two, and I had no chance to hug him.

My wife Kate and I are great kissers and huggers and touchers...with each other and with our family. I'll never forget the time, many years ago now, when a neighbor remarked, "Chris, every time I see you with your pup (Irish Setter), you have her in your arms. Have her feet ever hit the ground since you got her?" Recently a client gave me a button to pin on my jacket. She had it made for me, and the inscription read: "World's Greatest Hug Therapist." I was flattered, and at the same time, a bit embarrassed, as I realized how often I hug a client when he or she is leaving the office. For a while after that I wondered whether this was appropriate professional conduct. However, a voice inside kept saying, "Trust yourself, Chris." You know instinctively which people enjoy being touched and those who don't. So I keep hugging, discriminating as best I can. Happily, I find most people like to be hugged in one fashion or another.

I've come to discover there are several ways to hug. Some people, for instance, are comfortable with the full body hug, each hugger presses (to varying degrees) his or her body fully against the other. Then there is the bow hug. Each hugger sort of bows toward each other with the upper torsos (shoulders mainly) slightly touching. There is also the hip hug, which can be either both huggers hipping or one with the other full body. In either case, the hip is the point of contact, while the arms are perfunctorily placed on the shoulder. To each his own!

There are also a number of ways to kiss. There is the full lip kiss, the cheek or forehead kiss, even the ancient hand kiss. Naturally, if we are speaking of sexual relations *per se*, there are practically unlimited ways of kissing...all quite satisfying, so long as the people kissing agree.

Touching is really a fascinating skill; it can say so much so quickly as a form of non-verbal communication. It can frequently say better and faster what talking cannot. And when you combine touching with talking, you really have something going.

Not too long ago, Kate and I were having a cocktail before dinner. We had both just gotten home from work, a day that was tough on both of us. I casually mentioned I was attempting to set up a counseling session with two clients in my other office (out of state). Kate immediately jumped in and told me I should have called so-and-so first before contacting the other client. In an instant, I could feel my face flush with anger and hear myself saying to myself, "Who the hell is she to tell me how to run my business!" Then I began to go back at her. "Why do you think that? What are you really saying?" I could see her face begin to flush, and I knew we both were at trigger point.

Trigger point is where you can go either way—a blow up or a

cool down. I went inside myself again and asked, "What do you want? Warfare or a pleasant cocktail hour?" I then jumped up, walked over to Kate on the sofa, and gently rubbed her grimace into a smile. We laughed and had another cocktail, and discussed the important matters of the day.

There are people who want to kiss and hug and touch, yet they feel inhibited. One such person is Vera, a successful hair designer and salon owner in a large city. She is also an easy sexual quest, who goes from affair to affair, always hoping to find Mr. Right. She has no inhibitions when it comes to sexual relations, but she finds herself uptight when it comes to simply kissing, hugging, or touching another person, even her immediate family. Among her closer friends and family she is a puzzle. As a cousin confides, "She can jump in bed with the next guy who comes down the road, but she shrinks from kissing her own mother. She is like an ice cube!"

Vera acknowledges her cousin is correct. She can do the sexual routine, but don't ask her to show physical affection or attention to another, man or woman, apart from love making.

Vera is not alone in this seemingly paradoxical behavior. Many men and women I've counseled over the years fit this description. As one honest client put it, "In bed I'm a gymnast; out of bed I'm stiff as a board. I'd like to be more free with people, hug them, touch them, but I'm not, and I don't know why."

And of course there are those who are physically restricted in or out of bed, finding it so difficult to make physical contact with another person, regardless of who or where they are. They are uncomfortable kissing, hugging, touching. I feel sorry for them, because deep in their hearts, they want contact.

We all need and desire physical contact in one form or another. By nature, humankind reaches out for some connectedness in life. AT&T's "Reach Out and Touch Someone" is right on target. Reaching out, stretching toward another, is basic to human existence. As a picture is worth a thousand words, so a touch, a caress, a hug is often a thousand times more meaningful than words. After all, students of evolution have told us that way back when we started, we began with grunts, groans, and physical contact (not always the most pleasant or desirable) before we ever got to words.

A newborn infant hears the sounds and tones of her mother's voice and feels the warmth of her embrace. This is the language the child learns first—body language—and never really forgets it. How frequently we have heard the story of the abandonned infant placed in an institution, only to die soon after for lack of physical attention and affection.

For a successful corporate executive I know, his staff would march to hell and back, so great is their trust and loyalty. When asked the reason for their devotion, he replies: "We managers still find it so difficult to give a fair handshake or a pat on the back or a firm grip on the arm or even a hand around the shoulders or waist. In so many instances that is all it takes, and your co-workers will usually respond far beyond your expectations. The only thing is, make sure your touch is genuine. They know the difference."

Generally speaking, women seem to be more comfortable and therefore more accepting of physical affection and attention than males. Without going into the psychosexual development of males, it is sufficient to say that the fundamental reason for this male hesitancy can be laid at the feet of our cultural and social mores. Just as men don't cry or eat quiche, so they don't kiss, hug, or touch too much (and certainly not in public) unless they intend to go all the way. God forbid they should hug another man (family members excepted, sometimes).

Although some of this cultural and social restriction has gradually dissipated, you would be amazed at the number of times I encounter this in counseling sessions. She complains that he rarely touches her. He, in turn, defends himself by complaining that she ought to learn to stand on her own two feet and not need so much pampering. After all, there is a lot more to be concerned about in life besides making sure "she gets her buns pinched when I come into the kitchen from work."

I believe a good portion of our male population is confused about kissing, hugging, and touching. In fact, the only group of men who apparently are not confused are professional football players. If you watch football at all, you know what I mean when a touchdown is scored! Someday I fear someone will be smothered to death with all the hugging and touching that goes on in the end zone. Would that more married couples would react to each other like that, in a somewhat less enthusiastic fashion, of course, when one or the other has scored a "touchdown" at home or work, or some other place!

When the Sign of Peace was first introduced into the Roman Catholic Liturgy following the Second Vatican Council, people froze in their pews. The mere thought of making physical contact with a stranger sitting beside you sent chills up and down many worshippers' spines. I recall seeing people substituting a slight nod of the head and a self-consciously mumbled "peace" for a handshake, indicating their personal need to keep their distance. With time, however, like most things, this Sign of Peace has become standard fare in the liturgy. However, some would still prefer "to go to church to praise God, not to mingle with each other, shake hands and whisper a sweet little 'peace-be-to-you' to each other," as one disillusioned church-goer once told me.

I have never met a couple who were enjoying a mutually satisfying and lasting marriage who did not also enjoy touching each other with kisses, hugs and caresses, in or out of the kitchen. And what does it do for the relationship? I like the way Sean and Pelli answer this question.

Sean and Pelli have been growing a quality marriage for eleven years. Three years ago they were in counseling with me because of an escalating problem related to their financial status. Both were professional people making a very high combined income; they had one child and lived in an affluent community in a large city. The problem had to do with how to handle their money. Pelli was a saver, while her husband was a spender. Their differences led to arguments that led to fights that led to increasingly long periods of withdrawal and silence.

To this day, I am convinced that the major factor that enabled them to iron out their conflict was the physical connectedness they had developed through the years. Even when they were sitting in my office next to each other on the sofa, arguing their heads off, they were touching each other, most times in an unconscious reflex action. Sean would be trying to make a point, waving his right hand in the air, speaking loudly, almost into Pelli's face, and at the same time his left hand would be letting her know he cared. He would be caressing her shoulder ever so lightly. We call that unconscious anchoring.

A number of times Pelli displayed similar unconscious reactions to Sean, like putting her hand on his thigh while angrily telling him what she thought of his spendthrift ways!

At the conclusion of one session, an hour of particularly hostile exchanges, Sean spontaneously reached out for Pelli, and she instantly moved toward him. They were locked in an embrace for at least thirty seconds, tears moistening both their eyes.

During the following session, I called this behavior to their attention, noting from my observations over the weeks that they were really very touching individuals in spite of their differences. They readily agreed and went on to cite various instances where they automatically reached out to each other with kisses, hugs, caresses, touches of one kind or another. Sean said they loved to hold each other because it made them feel for the moment like they belonged to each other and no one else. Pelli commented that they often walk hand-in-hand in the woods while exercising their dogs and the feeling of oneness is sometimes almost ecstatic. They were both convinced that many of their arguments were detonated before they became fights because one or the other reached out for connectedness. I agreed it was difficult to argue with each other while you are hugging.

Sean and Pelli eventually resolved their conflict about money matters. They would be the first ones to admit it wasn't logic and reasoning about the issue that did the trick as much as it was their willingness to flip-flop and accommodate while lying in each other's arms.

This may sound romantically exaggerated, but Sean and Pelli explain it this way: "After [Chris] called our attention to the way we are always touching each other, even while we are arguing, we began to think and talk about it until what we knew all along in our heads actually became real to us, sort of in our whole beings, that we want to be inseparable. So we decided we'd better get this money thing straightened out fast. I guess you could say we suddenly became highly motivated. Nothing will stand in the way of our union."

Over the past decade or so, researchers in the field of human communication have discovered a number of strategies, skills, and techniques that elegant communicators use in their daily personal transactions that make them so effective as communicators. Interestingly enough, these people use these strategies, skills, and techniques largely on an unconscious level.[1] In other words, they just naturally do it. They are the charismatic personalities and we stand in awe at the manner and ease with which they communicate.

One of the skills and techniques they exhibit in their human transactions is what has become known as *anchoring*, which is really as old as the human race itself.[2] If you are even vaguely familiar with Pavlov's stimulus-response experiment with the dog and bell, you have a good idea of what anchoring is about. A simple example. Little Johnnie, in a fit of temper, strikes his baby sister. Mother witnesses what has transpired and does three things (actually a triple anchor of sorts). She shouts at Johnnie that he is a naughty boy (auditory anchor); her nostrils flare, her mouth twists into a grimace, and her eyes open wide as she stares at her son (visual anchor); and she picks him up and paddles him as he begins to cry (kinesthetic anchor).

Several days later Johnnie, his mother, and baby sister are in the family room. Johnnie again becomes irritated with his sister's behavior and raises his hand to strike her. As he does so he looks up at his mother and instantly recognizes the look on her face as she quietly stares at him. Immediately, he recalls his fate of a few days ago and drops his hand as mother's grimace turns into a smile, and he hears her words of praise for his loving patience with his little sister as she bends over and kisses him tenderly on the forehead.

A week passes and Johnnie is alone with his sister while mother is upstairs making the beds. Baby sister crawls over to where her brother is building a house with his blocks. She crawls too far and knocks over his building with her foot. Johnnie sees red, begins to lift his hand, then stops as he pictures his mother's face, hears her voice within, and internally feels once again the sting of her paddling him. There is another set of anchors he experiences almost simultaneously. He pictures her smile, hears her words of praise, feels her kiss, and decides to dart upstairs and tell his mother how patient he just was with his baby sister!

Anchors, of course, are not confined to little boys and baby sisters. Consciously or unconsciously, we resort to them all the time. People who are professional change agents, e.g., psychiatrists, psychologists, counselors, salespeople, teachers, etc., make frequent use of anchors (visual, auditory, kinesthetic) to help others retain knowledge or repeat behavior. It is very much a part of the learning process.

Not long ago, at the conclusion of a counseling session during which the client told an extremely painful story related to her impending marital breakup, it was obvious she was still quite distraught. Instinctively, I embraced her and held her for a moment or two, encouraging her to trust herself and the direction she was taking. She looked at me with tearful eyes and thanked me for hugging her. She said the instant I did it, she remembered her father doing it to her many years before whenever she came to him feeling down on herself or discouraged or afraid. As she went out the door, she turned to me, smiled, and softly remarked, "I think that did more good than the hour we just spent together."

Kissing, hugging, caressing, touching are kinesthetic anchors by definition, very powerful ones at that. How many times we forget exactly what a person has said to us, but we remember a hand on our shoulder, a tender kiss, an arm around our waist, a squeeze of the hand, fingers gently caressing our cheek, etc. And alas, how painful the absence of these anchors can be.

These kinds of kinesthetic anchors can bridge the I-Thou gap between two people as words alone can never do. A sincere kiss with a warm hug is the way Kate and I part company in the morning. The kiss and the hug is a morning ritual that is as much a part of our daily lives as getting dressed. Although we are a few miles apart during the day and our minds are attentive to our tasks, we feel a bond between us, a connectedness that has been anchored by way of our morning touch and go ritual.

Some couples have satisfying sexual relations even though the rest of their relationship is disintegrating. Upon closer examination, it is obvious that they are enjoying love making because it satisfies each of them individually, not because they are thus able to satisfy each other as well. One couple finds absolutely nothing in common with each other after fifteen years of marriage, except sex. He turns her on, and she does likewise for him. Outside of that, they go their separate ways. You would never catch them doing the touch and go routine. Couples in deep trouble don't kiss, hug, caress, touch each other. So, are they in trouble because of their lack of affection and attention, or did this lack arise out of the trouble they are experiencing in their relationship?

To me, couples whose marriages are quality relationships are so because a good bit of emphasis is placed on the day-to-day physical (and verbal, of course) demonstrations of affection and attention they manifest toward each other. Couples in troubled marriages usually have a history of neglect in this area. They may be great in bed, but then who can afford the luxury of staying in bed all day?

How little the cost of a touch and go, and how great the reward!

# Afterword

*Making Your Marriage Work* is not a novel to be read and put aside without further thought or emotions. It is a self-help book, a how-to type of book that will benefit you and your spouse immeasurably only if you commit yourselves to using it as a reference source that gives you detailed guidelines for growing a quality marriage. A few suggestions on how to use it are in order.

PART ONE - FUNDAMENTAL CONVICTIONS
The Latin adage, *Repetitio mater studiorum* (repetition is the mother of learning), can be aptly applied to the matter of developing and strengthening convictions. The more we meditate upon these convictions, the more we discuss them with our spouses and others, the more they will become imbedded in our thinking process. Webster defines conviction as a "settled persuasion." Meditation, and group discussions help greatly in persuading us as to the truth of a belief, and eventually our minds become settled in this truth. That's conviction.

Some questions that can be proposed for meditation and discussion are as follows:

- Do you view your marriage as an ongoing process rather than some once-and-for-all event?

- Do you overburden your marriage in terms of the happiness you expect?

- Is there a healthy amount of humor in your relationship?

- How are you at forgiving your partner?

- What is your track record like for accommodating your spouse?

- Do you flip-flop in your marriage?

- What is your attitude about sacrifice in marriage?

- How do you reduce stress in your marriage?

Proper attention through meditation and discussion will enhance your awareness of these fundamental convictions, convince you of their necessity for a quality relationship, and make them very much a part of your whole attitude toward marriage.


PART TWO - BASIC BEHAVIORS

There is only one way to develop and strengthen the basic behaviors discussed in the book: practice.

When I was a youngster, I wanted to play the piano. I used to envision myself as an orchestra leader with my piano at center stage and my musicians around me. People by the hundreds would crowd into gigantic music halls to dance and listen to my superb arrangements. I would become an internationally acclaimed entertainer in constant demand despite my astonishing fees.

My parents eventually bought my vision and then my piano and I started taking lessons...for about three months. During those few months I gradually awakened to the disappointing fact that practice does indeed make perfect. And for me, practice came to mean many hours learning to read music and coordinate hand and feet movement with keys and pedals, scales and notes, etc.

After two weeks, it all became very unexciting and the vision of grand musical success rapidly faded from my mind. Besides, all that practice was interfering with many other youthful pursuits that soon took priority over my piano lessons. Alas, within the year, my upright Steinway was sold to Johnnie Parker's parents. Apparently it was Johnnie's turn to have a vision.

Johnnie practiced and became a very fine musician. He never became an orchestra leader or concert pianist, but he created enough enthusiasm and love for playing that his eldest daughter took up the piano and is a concert pianist today.

The moral: Achievers succeed because they are willing to practice, to work at their goals. Julius Irving, former National Basketball Association superstar, made his play look easy. Bruce Springsteen, internationally known entertainer, appears as though he were born with a guitar on his hips and a song on his lips. Mary Lou Retton, Olympic Gold Medalist, seemed a natural at the 1984 games.

Each of these professional performers and many like them give the impression that what they do so well they do with the greatest ease. Not so, as we know. The hours spent working at their profession, their careers, and their jobs is mind boggling. Their commitment to practice, to enhance their skills, is awe-inspiring. Their awareness of the need to be continually vigilant and cautious in the pursuit of their goals is remarkable. Their sense of responsibility and the practices they undertake for the good of the whole is commendable, often quite courageous, and definitely necessary. Achievers in every sphere of human activity know that anything worth having is worth working for.

People enjoying quality marriages are achievers because they are in every sense of the word *practitioners of marriage.* They spend the required time and effort "at the piano," because they have a vision—to grow a quality relationship—and they are willing to give it top priority. They are committed to do whatever it takes to realize that vision.

I know of men and women who have resigned from lucrative positions in the professions, in business, industry, and education because they felt that kind of step had to be taken for the sake of their conjugal union.

People in quality marriages know that their quality does not come automatically. If you want to offer your spouse positive reinforcement, *then do it!* If you are convinced accommodation is the key to a quality marriage, then *accommodate!* If you want to become an effective listener in your marriage, then *practice* it! If you want to be a fair problem solver, then *work at it!*

If the path to a quality marriage sounds too simple, don't be deceived. The doing can take a great deal of effort, but anything worth having is worth working for. What you have to ask yourself is, "Is my marriage worth working for?"

It is my long-range hope and my continual prayer that *Making Your Marriage Work* will prove to be a book that will indeed help to send forecasters and demographers scurrying back to the drawingboard to correct downward the anticipated percentages of divorces and separations they presently predict will occur in the decades ahead. Wounded marriages can be healed. They can become quality marriages if only those husbands and wives in pain will attend to the basics of human relatedness.

I'll let you in on a secret. What this book is really doing is detailing and expanding a principle of human relationships proclaimed many centuries ago: "Do unto others as you would want them to do unto you."

# Notes

**CHAPTER ONE**

1. M. Scott Peck, M.D., *The Road Less Traveled* (New York: Simon and Schuster, 1978), p. 90.

2. Ignace Lepp, *The Psychology of Loving* (Baltimore: Helicon Press, Inc., 1963), p. 42.

3. Lepp, *The Psychology of Loving*, p. 42.

4. Peck, *The Road Less Traveled*, p. 91.

5. Abraham H. Maslow, *Motivation And Personality* (New York: Harper & Row Publishers, 1954), pp. 149-202.

6. Philip Blumstein and Pepper Schwartz, *American Couples* (New York: William Morrow, 1983), pp. 33-35.


**CHAPTER TWO**

1. Thomas J. Paolino, Jr., M.D. and Barbara S. McCrady, editors, *Marriage & Marital Therapy* (New York: Brunner/Mazel Publishers, 1978), pp. 1-12.

2. Eugene Kennedy, *The Pain of Being Human* (Chicago: Thomas More Press, 1972), p.p. 21-24.


**CHAPTER THREE**

1. Peck, *The Road Less Traveled*, p. 156.

2. Paolino and McCrady, *Marriage & Marital Therapy*, p. 6.


**CHAPTER FOUR**

1. *The New Webster's Comprehensive Dictionary of the English Language*, Deluxe Edition: (American International Press, New York: Delair Publishing, 1971).

2. N. Arthur Coulter, Jr., M.D., *Synergetics* (Englewood Cliffs, N.J.: Prentice-Hall, Inc., 1976), p. 27ff.

## CHAPTER SIX

1. Barbara B. Brown. *Supermind* (New York: Bantam Books, 1980), p. 84.

2. Brown, *Supermind*, p. 85.

3. Brown, *Supermind*, p. 93.

## CHAPTER EIGHT

1. Leslie Cameron-Bandler, David Gordon, and Michael Lebeau, *Know How* (San Rafael, Cal: Future Pace Books, Inc., 1985), 202 ff.

2. Kenneth Blanchard and Spencer Johnson, M.D., *The One Minute Manager* (New York: William Morrow, 1982), pp. 36-39.

3. Blanchard and Johnson, *The One Minute Manager*, p. 40. ff.

4. Thomas K. Connelan, *How To Grow People Into Self-Starters* (Ann Arbor: The Achievement Institute, Inc., 1980), p. 108, XIV.

## CHAPTER TEN

1. Vesta Kelly, *June 1982 Weekly Date Keeper* (Maywood, N.J.: Myron Manufacturing Corp., 1982), month of June.

2. Thomas Gordon, *Leader Effectiveness Training* (Wyden Books, 1971).

3. Christopher C. Reilly, *Put Your Ears On a Stick* (Reading, Pa.: People-Media, Inc., 1983) audiocassette.

## CHAPTER ELEVEN

1. Virginia Satir, *Peoplemaking* (Palo Alto: Science & Behavior Books, Inc., 1972), p. 72.

2. Joseph Yeager, "Pervasive Factors in Communication," A Paper (Newtown, Pa.: Eastern Neuro-Linguistic Programming Institute, no date, pp. 4-5.

CHAPTER TWELVE

1. Paul Hersey and Kenneth H. Blanchard, *Management of Organizational Behavior: Utilizing Human Resources* (Englewood Cliffs, N.J., Prentice-Hall, Inc., 1977), p. 84.


CHAPTER THIRTEEN

1. John Grinder and Richard Bandler, *Trance-Formations, Neuro-Linguistic Programming & the Structure of Hypnosis* (Moab, Utah: Real People Press, 1981).

2. Grinder and Bandler, pp. 61-63, 225-226.